WHY YOU SHOULD BE A SOCIALIST

Why you should be a socialist

Alan Maass

With an afterword by Howard Zinn

"Eugene V. Debs and the idea of socialism"

INTERNATIONAL SOCIALIST ORGANIZATION

 226-L

"Eugene V. Debs and the Idea of Socialism" reprinted here by permission of Howard Zinn and *The Progressive*.

Book designed and typeset by David Whitehouse.
Printed in the United States of America.

Maass, Alan.
Why you should be a socialist / Alan Maass
ISBN 0-935867-14-7

Alan Maass is the editor of *Socialist Worker*, newspaper of the
International Socialist Organization.

**The International Socialist Organization is linked to an
international grouping of socialist organizations:**

Australia: International Socialist Organisation
P.O. Box A338, Sydney South

Britain: Socialist Workers Party, P.O. Box 82, London E3 3LH

Canada: International Socialists
P.O. Box 339, Station E, Toronto, Ontario M6H 4E3

Cyprus: Ergatiki Demokratia, P.O. Box 7280, Nicosia

Denmark: Internationale Socialister, P.O. Box 5113, 8100 Aarhus C

Germany: Linksruck, Postfach 304 183, 20359 Hamburg

Greece: Socialistiko Ergatiko Komma
c/o Workers Solidarity, P.O. Box 8161, Athens 100 10

Holland: Internationale Socialisten
P.O. Box 92025, 1090AA, Amsterdam

Ireland: Socialist Workers Party, P.O. Box 1648, Dublin 8

New Zealand: Socialist Workers Organisation
P.O. Box 8851, Auckland

Norway: Internasjonale Socialisterr
Postboks 9226 Grønland, 0134 Oslo

Poland: Solidarnosc Socjalistyczna
P.O. Box 12, 01-900 Warszawa 118

Spain: Socialismo Internacional, Apartado 563, 08080 Barcelona

Zimbabwe: International Socialist Organisation
P.O. Box 6758, Harare

Contents

Introduction

Tom Martin was exhausted by 7 a.m. when his shift ended at the Goodyear tire factory in Gadsden, Ala. Goodyear was instituting a "continuous production" system to keep the 70-year-old plant running around the clock, and that meant all-night shifts and "flexibility" on work rules. Management said this would make the factory more competitive—more likely to survive in the new "globalized" economy. But Tom just felt more exhausted that February morning in 1999. He drove home and fell into bed.

Tom got a couple hours sleep before his wife called with the news. A local television station was reporting that Goodyear executives had decided to stop tire production in Gadsden. After 22 years of work, Tom Martin would be out of a job by the end of the year.

All day long as they arrived for their shifts, workers were shown a videotape of a company official saying that Goodyear regretted the decision to slash close to 1,400 jobs. But most, like Tom, had already heard. News of the layoffs spread fast in Gadsden, a small city of 43,000 in northern Alabama where almost everyone had friends or family who worked for Goodyear. "My son-in-law and people from my church work there," 69-year-old Willowdean Beard told a reporter from the *Gadsden Times*. "I don't know what Gadsden's going to do." Louise Godfrey worried about her husband David, a 22-year veteran of the plant who suffered a heart attack the year before. "He doesn't expect many places around here to hire a 50-year-old who's had a heart attack," Louise said.

The jobs that Goodyear was eliminating were good jobs—union jobs that paid a wage you could raise a family on. That's why Bob Fuller stayed at the plant for 23 years—the same place his father worked and his grandfather before that. But as the years went by, Bob found that his family's standard of living seemed to slip backward. The squeeze got worse in the 1980s when Goodyear asked for concessions to get through "tough times." Again in the 1990s, Goodyear asked for help—a $3-an-hour wage cut and more work-rule changes—and got it.

By the end of the decade, "tough times" were long over for Goodyear bosses—they were raking in profits of about $500 million a year on average. But that wasn't enough. So the jobs in Gadsden had to go.

As the months went by and the layoffs started, Tom and his coworkers tried to figure out how to get by. For many, it had been half a lifetime since they worked anywhere else.

Then came the surprise announcement in October. Goodyear management had made a mistake. It shut down the Gadsden factory based on a guess that demand for tires would fall during 1999. Wrong. Tire orders broke all records—and the company couldn't keep up with sales. It decided to reopen in Gadsden.

Tom Martin had his job back. But it wasn't quite the

same job. Now, Goodyear said, it was "temporary." The Gadsden factory would stay open only as long as demand for tires stayed high. At the beginning of the new year, management hinted that it might make the jobs permanent again—but only if the state government came up with $8 million to fix up the plant. State officials vowed to find the cash. But they admitted that even if they gave Goodyear an early Christmas, there was no guarantee that the factory would stay open if the economy changed—or even if the tire company's financial "experts" guessed completely wrong again.

So Tom Martin and his coworkers were "temps." They shared the same fate as millions upon millions of working people in the U.S. who can never be sure of the future. Whether it was packing its factories and offices with temps or slicing the jobs of veteran full-timers, Corporate America spent the last few years making sure people across the country lived in fear that they'd be next to go.

In the middle of what President Bill Clinton calls a "miracle" economy, life for the vast majority in the U.S. isn't miraculous at all. It's a life filled with more stress, longer hours, harder work—and less to show for it.

But if you found yourself on the other end of things—giving the orders, swinging the layoff ax, demanding the longer hours and harder work—than the last few years were a good time.

Just ask Anthony O'Reilly.

As the former CEO of food giant H.J. Heinz, O'Reilly was among the best-paid executives in Corporate America year after year during the 1990s. In addition to million-dollar salaries, O'Reilly got options to buy big chunks of Heinz stock. By the end of the decade, he'd built up a $750 million fortune.

But O'Reilly is best known in Corporate America for

showing his friends a good time. Every year, he threw a lavish three-day bash in Ireland—courtesy of Heinz. The guests were the crème de la crème from Wall Street, Washington and beyond. O'Reilly flew them in from around the world and put them up at the finest hotels. They dined and danced at formal balls held at O'Reilly's mansion and had track-side seats for the Heinz 57 Phoenix Stakes, a horse race held at Dublin's swank Leopardstown race track.

And while O'Reilly and his pals lived the high life in Ireland, Heinz's four division presidents—known within the company as the Four Horsemen of the Apocalypse—were hard at work on "Project Millenia," O'Reilly's plan for "cutting costs" by shutting down 25 factories worldwide and laying off thousands of workers.

Like Tom Martin, Anthony O'Reilly's job situation isn't clear. In 1998, he was pressured into resigning as CEO. But he has some options. As senior chairman of the board—a largely honorary position—he still has a plush 60th-floor office at Heinz's corporate headquarters in Pittsburgh. Or O'Reilly could look after his personal international business empire—he owns newspaper chains in Ireland and Australia, an oil-exploration company and the famous Irish china maker Waterford Wedgwood. If the weather gets cold, he can head for his mansion in the Bahamas. And O'Reilly's wife Chyrss—herself a Greek shipping heiress—spends time in France, where she owns one of the country's biggest stables of race horses.

Two years ago, O'Reilly bought his wife a token of his affection—a 40-carat diamond ring once owned by Jacqueline Kennedy Onassis. The ring cost $2.6 million. That's about what Tom Martin, David Godfrey and Bob Fuller *put together* earned in all their years of making tires for Goodyear.

These are the two worlds of the U.S. "miracle" economy.

Anthony O'Reilly lives in one, a world of privilege and power where he has the wealth to indulge any whim. Tom Martin belongs to a different world. It's a world of poverty and despair for large numbers of people. And even those who keep their heads above water have to struggle to make ends meet—fearing all the while that they'll be next when the likes of Anthony O'Reilly decide it's time to "cut costs."

Look beyond the borders of the U.S., and this tale of two worlds is even more extreme. More than 1.3 billion people around the world survive on less than $1 a day. Meanwhile, three executives from the Microsoft computer company—Bill Gates, Paul Allen and Steve Ballmer—are worth more between them than the combined economic output of the world's 43 least developed countries.

What could possibly explain this incredible gap between the pampered and privileged lives of a tiny few and the terrible poverty endured by billions of people every day?

Actually, Anthony O'Reilly doesn't really care. When he or any of the other fat cats at the top of this society make decisions, they have one goal above all others—to maintain and increase their wealth and power.

So when O'Reilly and his friends gather in Ireland or the Bahamas or some other paradise to toast their good fortune, they're also celebrating something else.

They're celebrating poverty and desperation and injustice.

Because it isn't simply that some people in the world are rich and some people are poor. The truth is that some people in the world are rich *because* other people are poor. People like Anthony O'Reilly are rich *because* people like Tom Martin have been driven all their lives to work harder for less—until they're kicked aside. Some people are rich *because* others go hungry, *because* others have nowhere to live, *because* others face the terror of war, *because* the future of the environment is put in jeopardy. That is the ugly truth about the capitalist society we live in.

More and more people know the reality of this ugly truth. And they are fed up.

When protests exploded during the World Trade Organization conference in Seattle at the end of 1999, even the mainstream media had to notice the growing numbers of people who weren't buying their happy talk. "They are folks who don't check each day to see how their 401(k) is doing or hang out with people who have become millionaires when their companies went public," the *Washington Post* reported. "What they all seem to agree on is that giant corporations have gone too far in gaining control over their lives and defining the values of their culture and that the WTO has become a handmaiden to those corporate interests."

Often in the past few years, this sentiment has remained below the surface, unnoticed amid the rejoicing about the "miracle" economy. But it has also welled up in struggles around the world—from the massive public-sector strikes in France in 1995 to the revolution against a corrupt U.S.-backed dictator in Indonesia in 1998 and beyond. These upheavals and countless others represent the growing rejection of a system that breeds poverty and war and environmental destruction.

There is an alternative—socialism.

Socialism is based on a few simple and straightforward principles. The world's vast resources should be used not to increase the wealth of a few parasites but to eradicate poverty and homelessness and every other form of scarcity forever. The important decisions about society shouldn't be left in the hands of people who are either rich or controlled by people who are rich but should be made by everyone democratically. Instead of a system that crushes our hopes and dreams, we should live in a world where we control our own lives.

These socialist principles have been part of a rich tradition of struggle against inequality and injustice—a struggle that is more relevant today than ever.

According to the United Nations, if the wealth of the world's seven richest men were redistributed, every single person on earth could be lifted out of poverty. Can there possibly be a good reason why this isn't done? If Bill Gates' billions could abolish hunger and disease right now, then what kind of a society would refuse to take the steps necessary to end the suffering?

It is a society that needs to be replaced—by socialism. The goal of this book is to show why—and how.

American Dream or American Nightmare?

Will your children live a better life than you?

For three decades following the Second World War, most people in the U.S. could answer "yes." That answer was the basis of what was known as the "American Dream"—the belief that working people and not just the rich could look forward to a steadily increasing standard of living and a better future for themselves and their children. Wages grew—not spectacularly, but enough so most families could afford more. Millions of young people became the first in their family to go to college. Diseases that plagued society for centuries were conquered. Rather than working until they dropped dead, people could look forward to retirement—when they could "enjoy life" after decades of hard work.

The American Dream was modest. It didn't change the fact that the Rockefellers and the Gettys led much better lives than anyone else, thanks only to the fact that they were born into wealth. And the dream didn't include everyone. African Americans, for example, remained second-class citizens, especially under the apartheid system of the Jim Crow South.

But for a majority of people in the U.S., the system of capitalism seemed to produce, if not spectacular wealth, than at least new benefits unknown to previous generations. Most people could hope to enjoy a better life as the years went by.

Today, the American Dream is over. For two decades, the majority of people in the U.S. have seen their living standards get worse, not better. Wages for most of the population have stagnated or fallen. Getting through college has become a huge financial burden. Most people work longer and harder than ever before—and yet their futures are less secure.

Rather than confidence about the present and hope for the future, working people in the U.S. today worry about holding on to what we have—and fear what the future will bring.

Working Harder for Less

Yet to hear the mainstream media tell it, Americans never had it so good. "They're shopping till they drop at the mall or on the Internet, happy as clams," *Business Week* magazine crowed at the beginning of 1999. Such talk is often accompanied by pictures of cigar-smoking, sports-utility-vehicle-driving yuppies. *Business Week* is right about them—they've never had it this good.

But for the rest of the U.S. population lower down the income ladder, the story is different. There may be computers and cell phones in more working-class households. But there are also more maxed-out credit cards—part of a household debt that's reached levels not seen since the Great Depression of the 1930s.

Strip away the media's impressions about the consumer spending boom, and it becomes clear that working people are having a harder time around most of the issues at the core of their lives. "Many problems that workers faced only in bad times have become fixtures at all times," the

New York Times admitted. "Some wages are still falling, people must be ready to work 12-hour shifts and six-day weeks, and no job is for keeps."

According to the Economic Policy Institute's "State of Working America" report, the median U.S. worker—that is, workers at the middle of the U.S. income ladder—earned 3.1 percent less in 1997 than they did in 1989 after accounting for inflation. Hourly wages either stagnated or fell for most of the bottom 60 percent of the working population.

So how have people kept their heads above water? By working much, much harder.

In 1998, median household income finally recovered to the level it was at a decade ago, after falling for much of the 1990s. But that's only because the average married couple in the U.S. worked 247 more hours a year—more than six extra weeks of full-time work per household. As the EPI concluded, "The typical American family is probably worse off near the end of the 1990s than it was at the end of the 1980s or the end of the 1970s."

Again, you'd never know it to judge from the media. Their impressions about the "miracle" economy usually begin by quoting the U.S. unemployment rate, which hit a 30-year low at the end of the 1990s. But there's another side to this statistic. Unemployment is low because—as President Clinton never tires of boasting—the U.S. economy produced millions of new jobs during the 1990s. But as one newspaper put it, "most of these jobs aren't worth waking up for." According to a 1998 study by the Jobs with Justice union coalition, 74 percent of the jobs that grew fastest in recent years pay less than a living wage—and 46 percent of them pay less than half a living wage. In the U.S. "miracle" economy, it's possible to work two and even three of these jobs—and still not earn enough to lift a family out of poverty.

Meanwhile, Corporate America has been slashing good jobs left and right. In 1998, corporate layoffs hit the highest point in a decade—higher even than the recession years of the early 1990s, according to the Challenger, Gray and Christmas consulting firm. Back then, mass layoffs were supposed to be necessary for an economic recovery. But by 1998, the U.S. economy was in the middle of one of its longest periods of uninterrupted growth in history. Profits had boomed for years, but Corporate America wanted more.

As the *Minneapolis Star Tribune* put it: "Layoffs used to be a sign of bad times in Corporate America. These days, job cuts are a signal that good times aren't good enough."

No wonder the fastest growing part of the workforce is the "working poor"—a concept that came of age in the 1990s. Of the 34 million people in the U.S. who live below the official poverty line, an incredible 15 million—almost half—live in households where one person works full time. According to a 1998 survey by the food-charity organization Second Harvest, well over one-third of the 26 million people who received help from food banks and shelters came from families where at least one person was working.

There's no doubt about where the money went, either. As *Business Week* bluntly pointed out: "From 1991 to 1997, workers' pay fell to the lowest share of national income since 1968, while the share going to profits rose to the highest level since that year."

Corporate America is raking it in. The 1980s was known as the "Decade of Greed" because of the huge transfer of wealth from the poorest to the richest in the U.S. But it turns out that the greed was just beginning. During the 1990s, the Wall Street casino continued to pay out big time for the fat cats. Meanwhile, according to a study conducted jointly by the Institute for Policy Studies and United for a

Fair Economy, compensation for top executives at America's biggest corporations increased at a rate of 50 percent a year during the 1990s. By contrast, after accounting for inflation, workers' wages rose at a rate of less than 1 percent a year for the decade. The resulting gap between the pay of top executives and the average factory worker is a staggering 419 to 1—10 times bigger than it was in 1980.

"No country without a revolution or a military defeat and subsequent occupation has ever experienced such a sharp shift in the distribution of earnings as America has in the last generation," the economist Lester Thurow summarized at the mid-point of the 1990s. "At no other time have median wages of American men fallen for more than two decades. Never before have a majority of American workers suffered real wage reductions while the per capita domestic product was advancing."

These facts barely register in all the happy talk about the economic good times we all supposedly enjoy. But they're very much a part of the lives led by the working majority in U.S. society. And they've contributed to a deep pool of bitterness and anger. The truth is that the American Dream exists only for the handful of the people at the top who've become fantastically rich at our expense. For everyone else, the American Dream is dead.

Sickness of the Health-Care System

Income and wealth aren't the only ways to measure the deteriorating quality of life for working people. Consider, for example, what happens when we get sick.

In terms of technology and resources, the U.S. has the most advanced health-care system in the world. Yet health care is a chronic source of fear and uncertainty for those lucky enough to remain healthy—and a nightmare for those who get sick.

The Wooldridge family knows this all too well. In late August 1995, Glenn and Jamie Wooldridge took their four-month-old daughter Elizabeth to the doctor because she wasn't gaining weight. "We thought it was just growing problems of a baby," Glenn later told KRON-TV in San Francisco.

But it wasn't "growing problems." Elizabeth's doctor suspected a serious lung disease called cystic fibrosis—and asked the Wooldridges' HMO for permission to perform a $128 "sweat test" to confirm the diagnosis. The request was denied. Two weeks later, Elizabeth ended up in the hospital, suffering from a 104-degree fever and what doctors guessed was pneumonia. Still, the HMO dragged its feet. It took three more days to approve a sweat test—which confirmed cystic fibrosis. But the information came too late. Elizabeth's condition grew worse, and on October 8, she died.

Sadly, the Wooldridges' ordeal with the health-care industry continues—because Elizabeth's older sister Aeranna was also diagnosed with cystic fibrosis. The Wooldridges have another health plan, but they still have to fight tooth and nail to get proper treatment. They face a maze of paperwork every time Aeranna visits a specialist—or needs a refill of one of the eight prescription medicines she takes. When doctors recommended a therapy vest connected to air pumps to help Aeranna breath, it took nine months to get insurance company approval.

"I can't describe it, I really can't," says Jamie. "You just do the same thing over and over again…That's the difference between then and now, but we didn't realize that at first with Elizabeth, and now we do. Until you're here, you think everything is fine. But when you're here, you realize how big of a hole you're in and how hard you have to fight to keep your children alive."

What a sick system that forces parents like Glenn and Jamie to "fight to keep their children alive." Yet horror stories like this one have actually become commonplace as "managed care" came to dominate the health-care industry during the 1990s.

"Mangled care" was supposed to be the solution to rising health costs. HMOs would cut out the waste and keep an eye on doctors who ordered unnecessary tests and procedures, saving consumers big money. But it was the HMOs that made the big money—by restricting care. Their philosophy was summed up by Richard Rainwater, cofounder of the for-profit HMO Columbia-HCA: "The day has come when somebody has to do in the hospital business what McDonald's has done in the fast-food business and what Wal-mart has done in the retailing business."

Ask almost anyone who's had contact with the health-care non-system in this country, and they'll tell you that they're sick of it. That includes health-care workers—even doctors—who have been under increasing pressure to cut corners on patient care to pump up the bottom line. Poll after poll show that a majority of Americans want a national health system that guarantees care for everyone. In fact, a 1998 *Wall Street Journal* survey found that more than half of those asked would be willing to pay $2,000 a year extra in taxes to guarantee health care for those who don't have access to it.

Yet Washington has only made the problem worse. Early in the 1990s, the Clinton White House gave up on comprehensive health-care reform—rather than alienate the powerful health-care bosses. Since then, the politicians have spewed some hot air about a few small-scale "reforms." Yet in 1999, Clinton and Congress couldn't even agree on a minimal patient bill of rights.

What exists in the U.S. today is really two health-care systems—one for the haves and one for the have-nots. For the rich, no expense is spared in using the latest techniques and technology on medical problems. For the rest, health care is "rationed." Drugs and treatments that could help people live longer, healthier and more fulfilling lives are often beyond reach because of a bewildering array of restrictions—imposed in the interests of the bottom line.

So it's no surprise that the most important factors determining a person's health have nothing to do with diet or exercise or smoking. The most important factors are social class and race.

The War on the Poor

The American Dream never did exist for one group of Americans—the poor. And if life has become more difficult for all working people, it is increasingly a disaster for the growing numbers thrown on the trash heap in the richest country in the world.

As of 1997, some 35.6 million people—close to one in seven Americans—lived below the official poverty line, according to the U.S. Census Bureau. That was a decline from 1993, the worst year in recent history. Yet more people were living in poverty at the end of the 1990s than at the beginning of the decade. Hunger and homelessness in the U.S. have grown worse—the direct result of cutbacks in government spending on poverty programs. The U.S. Conference of Mayors, for example, reported that requests for emergency food aid jumped by 16 percent in 1997 over the year before.

But statistics alone don't capture the terrors of being poor in the U.S. It's like walking through a mine field—where one false step can lead to catastrophe.

Just ask Janice Foster. In early 1998, she lost documents that she needed to remain on welfare. After her benefits were cut off, she fell behind on the rent, and in July, she and her three children were evicted. She began the ordeal that occupies all the time and effort of so many of the poor—trying to arrange a place to live for short periods with friends or relatives or in down-and-out hotels.

By August, she had failed. Janice and her children ended up at the Union Rescue homeless shelter in the middle of Los Angeles' Skid Row—a human dumping ground on the edge of the city's downtown. There, in the shadow of fancy skyscrapers, 3-year-old Deon and his 14-year-old brother William play in alleys—among men sleeping in cardboard boxes and using drugs in the doorways.

There are plenty of well-fed academics who claim to understand all this—why people like Janice and her children have gone through hell. "If poor people behaved rationally, they would seldom be poor for long in the first place," New York University political science professor Lawrence Mead told author Jonathan Kozol.

Smug words. But among the millions of people with stories like Janice's, there is little "irrational" about anything they did. The only thing irrational is the miserable circumstances they were forced to deal with in the first place. "If only I could, I would have done things differently," Janice told a *New York Times* reporter, thinking back on the events that landed her and her family on Skid Row. "I would have saved more money. But really, I didn't have any money to save."

Yet blaming the poor for being poor is at the heart of everything the politicians have done about poverty during the 1990s. In August 1996, President Clinton signed federal legislation to "reform" the welfare system that people like Janice relied on to survive. The welfare "reform" bill abolished the federal government's main welfare program, Aid to Families with Dependent Children. But it didn't stop there. It slashed $54 billion over six years from all kinds of programs—from food stamps to Supplementary Security Income for disabled children.

According to the Urban Institute, the poorest one-fifth of American families lose an average of $1,310 each year in benefits of all sorts as a result of the 1996 law. That's the difference between hard times and destitution for millions of people.

It's hard to overstate how mean-spirited these cuts are. When former House Speaker Newt Gingrich (R-Ga.) and his fellow Republican thugs tried to justify cuts in the SSI program, they claimed that disabled children were coached by their parents to fake crippling diseases. "[Children are] being punished for not getting what they call crazy money, or stupid money," Gingrich actually told reporters in 1995. "We are literally having children suffering child abuse so they can get a check for their parents."

As vile as this kind of talk is, the consensus in Washington is that welfare "reform" worked. Clinton considers it a high point of his presidency. "The welfare rolls have been cut in half," Clinton gushed on the third anniversary of welfare "reform" in 1999.

The number of people receiving welfare benefits *is* lower. But a 1999 study by the Urban Institute found that only 60 percent of recipients who left the welfare rolls had jobs when they were interviewed. And even those who were working didn't have much of a future to look forward to. The average wage for former recipients was $6.61 an hour—not enough to keep a family of three above the poverty line. About half said they had skipped a meal to make food last until the end of the month, and 40 percent said they couldn't pay rent, mortgage or utility bills at least once in the previous year.

And as welfare rights activists point out, the worst is yet to come. The full consequences of welfare "reform" have been hidden by low unemployment and the expanding economy. There's no telling what will happen when a recession hits—with the social safety net slashed to pieces.

The Politics of Scapegoating

In mid-February 2000, the U.S. passed a terrible new milestone. It locked up its 2 millionth inmate in a jail or prison.

More Americans are behind bars today than live in the cities of San Francisco, Boston and Denver combined. The U.S. imprisons a higher proportion of its population than any country in history, according to the November Coalition. With just 5 percent of the world's population, the U.S. accounts for one-quarter of the world's prisoners.

To judge from these statistics, you'd assume that crime was running wild in the U.S. Not true. Crime rates in virtually every category—including violent crime—decreased during the 1990s. There's only one explanation for the sky-rocketing prison population—the politicians' "tough on crime" hysteria. Law-and-order rhetoric is an easy button to push in an election campaign. From the White House on down, the politicians have competed to propose legislation that will crack down harder on criminals—no matter how insignificant the crime.

Take California's "three-strikes-and-you're-out" law, under which defendants must be sentenced to 25 years to life if they're convicted of a third felony, no matter how serious. Michael Riggs is one of its victims. He got a 25-year sentence for stealing a bottle of vitamins from a supermar-ket—a "crime" that a state appeals court admitted was "motivated by homelessness and hunger" even as it upheld the sentence. And Riggs isn't alone. California has locked up 40,000 people under the 1994 law for second and third strikes—about a quarter of the state's prison population.

There's another sick aspect to California's three-strikes law—some 75 percent of three-strikes victims are non-white, twice their percentage in the state's overall popula-tion. This reflects the U.S. injustice system as a whole. For example, according to The Sentencing Project, African Americans are 13 percent of drug users in the U.S., but they account for 35 percent of arrests for drug possession, 55 percent of convictions for possession and 74 percent of those sentenced to prison for possession.

For most of the people warehoused in U.S. prisons, their real crime is being poor or having the wrong skin color. This reality is plainest in the most barbaric face of the justice system—the death penalty. African Americans account for 43 percent of prisoners on death row, almost four times their percentage in the overall U.S. population. More than 90 percent of defendants charged with capital crimes are too poor to afford an experienced lawyer to rep-resent them. The result has been an epidemic of cases of innocent people going to death row, framed by racist cops and fanatical prosecutors.

In Washington, D.C., young men from poor African Amer-ican neighborhoods stand almost a 50-50 chance of being under the supervision of the criminal justice system—either behind bars, on parole or on probation. Imagine the turmoil if the statistics were even remotely similar in one of the bet-ter-off, predominantly white areas of D.C. or its suburbs.

Could there be a clearer illustration of the effects of

racism in U.S. society? Many commentators talk today about how racial divisions are being overcome. And in fact, opinion polls show that personal attitudes about race have become much more liberal. But institutional racism still runs very deep. Aside from a small minority of middle-class African Americans who got the most benefits out of the reforms won by the 1960s civil rights movement, living conditions for the majority of Blacks aren't much better than they were 30 years ago. African Americans still regularly face terror at the hands of police forces steeped in racism. Unemployment for Blacks runs at twice the rate of the population as a whole, and African Americans are less likely to go to college.

We're told that America is the "land of opportunity"—that no matter where you start, if you work hard, you can make something of yourself. But America looks very different from the poverty-stricken, inner-city neighborhoods of this country. From there, it seems like no matter how hard you work, if you're Black and poor, you don't stand a chance.

Ultimately, this terrible human waste is a price that the politicians are willing to see us pay. They may make pious statements about tolerance and justice. But the system they preside over thrives on racism. For politicians, issues like crime provide scapegoats that shift attention away from the real problems they do nothing about—like our crumbling schools or health care, to name two. And that's more valuable to a politician than all the lives of people sent away for trivial offenses.

Scapegoating has a history as old as capitalism—for the simple reason that our rulers have to keep us divided in order to conquer. But more and more people see through the lies. The obvious fact is that we live in a class society— a world divided between the haves and have-nots.

New World Disorder

It was February 1991, and U.S. and allied warplanes were pulverizing Iraq in the most intense bombing campaign in the history of war. That was the moment that President George Bush chose to explain his vision for the world's future.

The Gulf War against Iraq was proving that America was the world's sole military superpower. And the collapse of the former USSR and its Eastern European empire had put an end to the Cold War rivalry between "democracy" in the West and so-called "socialism" in the East. The U.S.-style free market was triumphant—everyone in the media said so. So as the military annihilation of Iraq came to a close, Bush declared that a new era had begun—that the U.S. would preside over a "new world order" of peace and prosperity.

Nearly a decade later, Bush's rhetoric seems like a cruel joke.

According to the United Nations' *Human Development Report* for 1999, income per person in half the countries of the world was *lower* at the end of the 1990s than at the beginning. Among the three-quarters of the world's population that lives in developing countries, more than half lack access to safe sewers, one-third don't have clean water, one-quarter lack adequate housing and one-fifth have no modern health services of any kind.

Whole areas of the globe seem to have been left to die by the capitalist system. In the desperately poor countries of sub-Saharan Africa, for example, the average household consumes 20 percent less than it did two decades ago. One out of every five children there dies before their fifth birthday, and half the population lives below the poverty line.

In some countries, society is simply unraveling. Take Zambia, a country the size of Texas in central southern Africa. A dramatic fall in the world price for copper tore the heart out of the economy during the 1990s, and the result has been outright barbarism. Life expectancy in Zambia has dropped to 37 years old, less than half what it is in the U.S. Half of the country's children are chronically malnourished, and child mortality rates have jumped by 20 percent in 10 years.

This is a direct consequence of a free-market system that benefits copper-buying multinational corporations and Zambia's own corrupt rulers at the expense of everyone else. And as if it weren't sick enough that human lives are at stake every time the price of copper falls, the bankers of the world's richest countries are trying to finish off Zambia.

Zambia owes a huge foreign debt that it can never repay. Yet for years, the government spent hundreds of millions on debt repayment to the West—$1.3 billion between 1990 and 1993, 35 times what it spent on primary school education. At the end of the 1990s, Western leaders came up with a plan to forgive debts in some of the world's poorest countries. But there was one big string attached—

countries like Zambia had to keep obeying orders from the International Monetary Fund and the World Bank.

The IMF and the World Bank are international financial institutions set up by the U.S. They control whether poor countries receive economic aid—and therefore, they have a blackmailer's power to demand the government policies that they consider "appropriate."

During the early 1990s, IMF and World Bank officials decided that the government-run sector of Zambia's economy was "bloated"—too much government spending, too many programs to help the poor, too much intrusion of the government into the free market. The solution? One of the IMF's notorious "structural adjustment programs." The Zambian government was ordered to sell off state-run companies and services—including the crucial copper industry—to private buyers and slash government spending.

It's hard to imagine policies that could have done *more* damage. Zambia sold off state-run companies at a record pace, but half the newly privatized firms are bankrupt. According to human rights expert Mark Lynas, more than 60,000 workers lost their job as a direct result of structural adjustment—plunging up to half a million Zambians into outright destitution.

Masauso Phiri, who lives in one of the shantytowns that ring the capital of Lusaka, wonders if there's any point to going on. He lost his job as a security guard in the wave of layoffs that followed implementation of the IMF's structural adjustment program. "I know it's meant to put the economy on the right track," Masauso told Lynas. "But to me, it seems to make us suffer. We can't eat policies. I don't have any hope. I don't have any money, so I can't think of any future. My future is doomed."

Masauso is only one victim of the free market out of literally billions around the world. A couple decades ago, it might have seemed like the worst flash points of poverty in the world were in remote regions untouched by the modern economy. That isn't the case today. It's not unusual, even in central Africa, to find modern factories built by Western corporations side by side with miserable shantytowns—because the jobs don't pay a living wage.

The U.S.-based multinational Nike has 17 factories in the Southeast Asian country of Indonesia, pumping out an average of about 7 million pairs of shoes a month. In 1997, when the legal minimum wage in Indonesia leapt to $2.47 a day, Nike bosses started having second thoughts. "There's concern what that does to the market—whether or not Indonesia could be reaching a point where it's pricing itself out of the market," said company spokesperson Jim Small. Fortunately for Nike, Indonesia was plunged into a severe financial crisis, and the legal minimum fell as low as 50 cents a day.

Today, Indonesian workers who produce shoes for the immensely profitable Nike are among the 1.3 billion people in the world who survive on less than $1 a day.

Across the globe, the free market has produced more misery and suffering, not less. This is especially obvious in Eastern Europe. In 1989, masses of people rebelled against the so-called "socialist" regimes of Eastern Europe, toppling one government after another in a matter of weeks. The revolutions were touted as the triumph of the free market. Western-style capitalism was supposed to end the poverty and tyranny of the old state-run systems.

In reality, the old Eastern European regimes had nothing to do with genuine socialism. They were run by dictatorial governments that organized society through state control of the economy rather than Western-style private ownership. And in fact, after the 1989 upheavals got rid of a few hated figureheads, most of the people running the new system had been bosses under the old one—from factory managers who became the new private owners to police forces that emerged almost intact. The change in Eastern Europe was not from socialism to capitalism but rather from one form of capitalism to another—state capitalism to Western-style market capitalism.

With the same crooks presiding, new governments imposed harsh free-market "reforms"—and sent their economies plummeting. In Russia, living standards collapsed for most people—while a corrupt and violent elite got filthy rich. In August 1998, Russia defaulted on its government debt, and the economy nose-dived even deeper. One year later, between 30 and 40 million people lived below the official poverty line of $30 a month, and 90 percent of Russians said their primary job didn't pay enough to keep up a decent standard of living.

So much for a "new world order" of prosperity.

Wars Without End

Bush's promise of a new era of peace hasn't worked out either. In the decade since February 1991, not one day has passed in which the U.S. government has not had military forces committed around the world in one conflict or another.

Wars continue to rage across the globe. In 1994, Central Africa was the site of one of the bloodiest episodes of the new world order—the genocide of as many as 1 million Tutsis in Rwanda. The echoes of that slaughter are still being heard today in an ongoing war involving some of the world's poorest countries—Rwanda, Congo, Uganda, Zambia, Angola and Zimbabwe. In Asia, India and Pakistan—countries that had recently tested nuclear weapons for the first time—went to the brink of all-out war in 1999 over Kashmir, a small mountainous region that both claim. And in Latin America, the U.S. is helping the Colombian government step up its 40-year-old dirty war against left-wing rebels.

U.S. politicians usually try to distance themselves from violence and war. They're the products of age-old ethnic or religious rivalries, we're told. But the truth is that the U.S. war machine has a hand, directly or indirectly, in stoking many of the military conflicts around the world—sometimes supplying advice, sometimes the guns and sometimes the soldiers.

Of course, when the Pentagon gets directly involved in a war, then the explanations change. U.S. war aims are always "humanitarian." We're told that America goes to war to preserve peace or protect democracy.

Take the NATO war against Yugoslavia in 1999. President Clinton and other Western leaders said they were intervening to stop Serbia from driving ethnic Albanians out of Kosovo. But NATO bombing provided Yugoslav President Slobodan Milosevic with the cover to step up "ethnic cleansing." Kosovar Albanians who fled Serbian attacks and NATO bombs were left to rot in squalid camps while the Western powers refused to accept any but a token number of refugees. And once the war was over, NATO "peacekeepers" looked the other way as Albanians drove the minority Serb population out of Kosovo.

Clinton also claimed that NATO forces had no quarrel with ordinary Serbs—and would target only Milosevic's military machine. That was a bald-faced lie. In order to win the war, NATO warplanes hammered Serbian cities mercilessly, leaving military units almost untouched—and ordinary Serbs to bear the brunt of the devastation.

After NATO's "humanitarian" intervention, the Balkans are more unstable than ever. No one knows how many people will die in the years to come as victims of the unexploded cluster bombs that litter Serbia and Kosovo or the environmental catastrophe caused by the bombardment. The main winner in this war was the U.S. government—which proved that it had the military might to remain the world's top cop.

Meanwhile, as bombs were falling on Belgrade in the spring of 1999, the U.S. continued to wage a savage war on Iraq.

According to the UN, more than 1.5 million Iraqis have died since the 1991 Gulf War. Only a minority were victims of bombs and guns. By far the majority died lingering and terrible deaths as a result of UN sanctions backed up by the U.S.

Sanctions have reduced one of the most advanced societies in the Middle East to the level of poverty of the poorest countries in the world. The most basic goods—medicine, textbooks, fertilizer, chemicals for sanitizing water—are barred from reaching the country. Since sanctions were first imposed, food prices have increased by 50 times. Ordinary Iraqis get only about one-third the amount of food necessary to meet basic nutritional requirements. UN officials describe epidemics of diseases caused by parasites which ought to be easily treatable—except that hospitals in Iraq are chronically short of medicine and filled with broken-down equipment.

There is no other way to describe this U.S. war except as genocide.

And what is the justification? The Iraqi people have been put through hell because the U.S. government wants to get rid of Saddam Hussein. This is the same dictator who came to power after a CIA-backed coup in 1963. U.S.

officials had no problems with Saddam when they handed over lists of Iraqi socialists to be hunted down and massacred by his Ba'athist Party regime. The U.S. backed Iraq when Saddam went to war against Iran in 1980, and it looked the other way when he used chemical weapons against the Kurdish minority in Iraq.

U.S. policy changed only after Saddam invaded Kuwait in 1990—threatening the flow of Middle East oil. "If Kuwait grew carrots, we wouldn't give a damn," one former White House official admitted in the run-up to the war. President Bush, too, was honest about why the U.S. was ready to slaughter innocent Iraqis. "We need the oil," Bush said as U.S. warships steamed toward the Persian Gulf. "It's nice to talk about standing up for freedom. But Kuwait and Saudi Arabia aren't exactly democracies."

The motives of the U.S. government in military conflicts couldn't be put more plainly. This has been true since the U.S. emerged as a world power a century ago with its victory over Spain in the Spanish-American War. Even then, war supporters in Washington justified the fighting with rhetoric about liberating the subjects of Spain's colonial domination in the Caribbean and the Pacific. But the real aim of the U.S. was to be the new colonial boss—which is what it became in the former Spanish possessions of Cuba, Puerto Rico, the Philippines and Guam.

The U.S. was late among the world's main powers in starting an empire, but it made up for that in violence. It started out in its own "backyard"—Latin America. Over the last century, U.S. troops have invaded Cuba five times, Honduras four times, Panama four times, the Dominican Republic twice, Haiti twice, Nicaragua twice and Grenada once.

Eventually, American troops spread out around the world—conquering less powerful nations but also fighting with other powerful countries over which would control what parts of the globe. The conflicts were both economic and military, but these empire-building—or imperialist—adventures never had anything to do with democracy and freedom. The goal was always the same—protect and extend the power of U.S. rulers.

Gen. Smedley Butler's beat was Latin America. As a Marine Corps officer in the opening decades of the 20th century, he headed a number of U.S. military interventions. Butler was under no illusion about what he was doing:

> I spent most of my time being a high-class muscle man for Big Business, for Wall Street and for the bankers. In short, I was a racketeer for capitalism…Thus, I helped make Mexico and especially Tampico safe for American oil interests in 1914. I helped make Haiti and Cuba a decent place for the National City Bank to collect revenues in…I helped purify Nicaragua for the international banking house of Brown Brothers in 1909-1912. I brought light to the Dominican Republic for American sugar interests in 1916. I helped make Honduras "right" for American fruit companies in 1903.

Colin Powell may not be as honest about it, but U.S. imperialism is no more kindly or charitable than it was in Butler's time. Countries like the U.S. don't go to war to stop tyrants or any of the other "humanitarian" reasons the politicians like to talk about. They go to war to preserve and extend their economic power.

When weaker countries like Iraq and Yugoslavia step out of line—by directly threatening a vital economic interest like Middle East oil or by indirectly threatening the political balance of power in an economically important region—the U.S. and the world's other major powers will try to impose their domination. But the 20th century has also seen two horrific world wars—not to mention dozens of smaller conflicts—because of battles *between* the major powers. At their root, these wars were also about economic power—about which imperialist country would dominate which areas of the globe.

Wars are a constant feature in the history of capitalism. They are the product of the ruthless competition for profit at the heart of the free-market system—the result of economic competition between bosses growing into political and military competition.

That's why wars are inevitable under capitalism. Inevitable, that is, unless ordinary people fight back against the violence—and against a system that breeds war.

The Madness
of the Free Market

In June 1999, Bill Gates gave away $5 billion to support education causes—at the time, the largest-ever charitable contribution from a living person. Mighty generous. But Gates didn't even miss a part of his vast fortune. About a month after he announced the gift, a rumor on Wall Street sent the price for Microsoft stock soaring. In a matter of a few hours, Gates, who owns about one-fifth of Microsoft's stock, made back the whole $5 billion he gave away.

That $5 billion bounce pushed Gates' personal fortune past the $100 billion mark. Though he slipped back some in the following months, Gates is still far and away the world's richest man, with twice as much wealth as number two—investor Warren Buffet, who was worth just $42.5 billion when Gates set the new milestone.

Wealth on this obscene scale is mind-numbing. But think of it this way: Imagine we had a full year's wages for an average U.S. factory worker—$29,267 in 1998, according to the Labor Department—in stacks of $20 bills. If we laid all the bills end to end, they would stretch 731 feet. That's a little more than one-eighth of a mile—about one city block or half a lap around a football field.

Now imagine we had Gates' fortune in $20 bills. If we laid them end to end, they would stretch 473,484 *miles*. That's back and forth between New York and Los Angeles 168 times. At its high point, Gates' fortune literally stretched to the moon and back again.

Gates may be ahead of the pack, but the rest of the astronomically rich are doing better than ever, too. According to the United Nations, the world's richest 225 people saw their wealth double between 1994 and 1998. Together, they're worth more than $1 trillion—roughly equal to the total annual income of the poorest one-half of the world's population.

That's 225 people with more money than 3 billion people.

What could this tiny elite have done to deserve so much more than anyone else? We're often told that they worked for their fortunes. And at first glance, this might seem to apply to Gates, who wasn't born into billions.

But how did he get so rich? Did he work 3 million times harder than anyone else? Is he 3 million times smarter or 3 million times more enterprising? No. Bill Gates is rich because his company gained control of computer software developed by other people and successfully marketed it as the boom in personal computers took off in the 1980s. In other words, he was lucky.

E. Pierce Marshall, on the other hand, was lucky in a different way. He was lucky enough to be born the second son of oil baron J. Howard Marshall. And he was even luckier when his father died, leaving him a billion-dollar fortune. Pierce never had to do a day of work in his life—aside from squabbling with his brother and assorted other freeloaders over the loot. Yet E. Pierce Marshall has more money than 100,000 minimum-wage workers make in a year of full-time work.

The truth is that the rich do nothing special to deserve having so much more than anyone else. In fact, they typically do nothing much at all. They almost never have anything to do with actually making or distributing products that people buy. For example, Bill Gates doesn't assemble or package or transport or sell Microsoft products. He doesn't even come up with the software. Gates is rich because he's *owns*. He and his fellow Microsoft shareholders own the means of producing computer software—the factories and offices, the machines, patents on different technologies.

This is true about capitalism generally. A small class of people who own the "means of production" hire much larger numbers of people to do the actual work of making or providing different goods or services. No wealth would exist without their labor. The oil that's the source of E. Pierce Marshall's fortune, for instance, would still be in the ground.

For their labor, workers get paid a wage—higher or lower depending on the demand for their skills, whether they're in a union and so on. But workers are never paid as much as they produce—usually, they're paid far less. The employers get to keep what's left over after they've covered wages and other costs of production such as raw materials and machinery. This amount of money that they skim off for themselves is profit.

This is supposed to be fair—that workers get a "fair day's wage for a fair day's work," and employers get a reasonable return on their investment. But there's nothing fair about it. The employers have all the advantages. They have all sorts of methods to keep wages down. But there's no limit on their profits. Capitalism is built around organized theft—the theft of the value of what workers produce by the people who employ them.

The term that socialists use to describe this is exploitation. That word is usually associated with especially low wages and terrible conditions. But exploitation goes on all the time. Every minute of the working day, a small class of people who do no productive work gets richer because they control the goods and services produced by people who do work. And of course, it follows that if these bosses can get workers to work harder or accept lower wages, they can keep even more money for themselves.

So as individuals, Bill Gates and E. Pierce Marshall may be lucky. But the social class they belong to—the ruling capitalist class—doesn't rely on luck. It relies on a system organized around stealing the wealth created by the vast majority—the working class.

Poverty in a World of Plenty

Inequality isn't new. There have been rich and poor for thousands of years. What's different about the world today—as compared to, for example, the world our ancestors lived in 200 years ago—is that the resources exist to end poverty immediately. The UN estimates that it would take $40 billion a year to fund basic education, health care, adequate food and safe water for everyone in the world. Bill Gates could pick up the tab himself and still be the richest man in the world.

Yet terrible poverty continues to exist alongside incredible wealth. The reason is that capitalism is designed to protect the rich and increase their wealth—no matter what the human cost.

Take the example of food production. According to the *State of the World's Children 1998* report issued by the United Nations Children's Fund, more than 6 million children under the age of five will die this year of malnutrition and its related diseases. The number 6 million has a terrible significance in the modern world—that is the number of Jews murdered by Germany's Nazis in the Holocaust during the Second World War. A Holocaust of the world's children takes place every year—because of hunger.

What could be the cause of such a horror? Has there been some worldwide war of devastation or an international natural disaster that makes it impossible to produce enough food to go around?

In fact, the opposite is true. There's enough food *in storage* today to feed all the people in the world. And this is food that already exists. According to one study, if the useable land of the world were cultivated effectively, the earth could feed more than 40 billion people—far more than are ever likely to inhabit the planet.

The food exists. So there must be a problem in getting it to the desperately poor people around the world who need it. Again no. Such a rescue effort wouldn't be beyond the capabilities of the world's most powerful countries. During the Gulf War against Iraq, for example, the U.S. government and its allies spent $1 billion a day pouring troops, equipment, supplies and weapons into the Persian Gulf. If the U.S. could mobilize this kind of operation to batter a small country into submission, surely it could carry out an effort to save the lives of 6 million children.

The sick reality is that, instead of being organized to feed the hungry, the system of capitalism is organized around *not* feeding everyone. The owners and executives who control food production have an interest in keeping up prices—and therefore profits. That means limiting the amount of food for sale. When there's too much food for sale, prices and profits fall. So the food bosses have convinced governments around the advanced world to store "surplus" food. In a world in which 6 million children starve to death, one-fifth of all food produced in the U.S. is either stockpiled, bulldozed or burned.

As the *Financial Times* newspaper admitted: "People are not hungry these days because food supplies are not available; they are hungry because they are poor."

Profits come before people at every step of the way. Before popular pressure forced them to give up on the scheme, the corporate giant Monsanto and the U.S. Department of Agriculture had some of the world's finest scientific minds at work developing crops that would kill their own seeds. The goal was to prevent farmers from gathering seeds after harvest and using them for replanting the next year. Instead, the bosses wanted farmers to buy more seed. "Seed saving is a tradition in much of the world," reported the *Washington Post,* "but the practice makes it difficult for seed companies to recoup their research and development costs." Put another way, Monsanto and the other agribusiness giants were willing to put more burdens on the Third World's 1 billion subsistence farmers—in order to increase their profits.

The German poet Bertolt Brecht might have had this science-fiction-comes-to-life scenario in mind when he wrote: "Famines do not simply occur—they are organized by the grain trade."

In the same way, you can say that poverty and inequality don't simply occur. They are organized by a tiny class of rulers at the top of society that benefits from the whole setup—that increases its wealth and power at the expense of the rest of us.

A System Gone Mad

For defenders of the free-market system, there's a simple response to Brecht's point: Dismiss it as a conspiracy theory. After all, talk about "famines" being "organized by the grain trade" seems like something out of the "X-Files" —shadowy figures in back rooms hatching plots to dominate the world.

Actually, "conspiracies" take place every day in Corporate America. For example, in August 1998, three top executives of the agribusiness giant Archer Daniels Midland— the self-proclaimed "supermarket to the world"—were found guilty of working with the company's "competitors" to fix the international price for lysine, a widely used additive for animal feed. The ADM bosses were caught red-handed on FBI videotapes that showed them meeting in posh hotels with the executives of other companies to plan out their price-fixing scheme—and laughing about it.

Still, capitalism doesn't depend on conspiracies. Poverty and inequality are built into the structure of the system itself.

In theory, the capitalist free market is supposed to work according to the law of supply and demand. The basic idea is that capitalists control what gets produced and how, but they make their decisions according to what people buy. So consumers use their dollars as a sort of "vote"—and capitalists compete with each other to provide the products that consumers "vote" for.

But there's a problem at the heart of this theory: What if you don't have any money? Then you don't get a vote— and capitalists won't produce what you want.

In order for the free market to produce what's needed for everyone in society, there would have to be a roughly equal distribution of dollars to "vote" with. But in the real world, the rich have far more "votes" than anyone else. So the system is bound to put a priority on making products to meet their needs, rather than the needs of the whole society.

The result is a world where whole industries are devoted to products and services that are a total waste. Take advertising. Very few people care passionately about the difference between 7-Up and Sprite. But the owners and executives at the companies that produce the two soft drinks do—their profits depend on it. So they spend enormous sums trying to convince people to buy one over the other.

7-Up's 30-second-long ad during the 1999 Super Bowl cost $1.6 million—which is about as much as a decently paid Teamster driver for 7-Up will earn in a lifetime of work.

And advertising is one of the more harmless forms of waste. Governments around the world spend $780 billion each year on the means to slaughter people—and ultimately to destroy the planet.

Every year, the U.S. government spends billions of dollars on what one government official described as an attempt "to hit a bullet with another bullet at 15,000 miles per hour." That's the reality of the anti-ballistic missile defense system named Star Wars by President Ronald Reagan and the right-wing kooks who first proposed it two decades ago. Since then, the U.S. has plunged some $55 billion down this rat hole—and has yet to produce any evidence that Star Wars could even work. Nor is there any evidence that the U.S. faces a threat for a missile defense system to guard against. None of the supposed "rogue" nations mentioned by tough-talking politicians are in a position to launch intercontinental missiles for a Star Wars system to shoot at.

So why does the Pentagon keep squandering the money? There's one obvious answer, of course. Filthy rich military contractors like Lockheed Martin and Raytheon depend on boondoggles like Star Wars, and they spend plenty of money at election time to make sure that their servants in

Washington don't interfere with the Pentagon gravy train.

But even when the weapons work, military spending is a colossal waste from the point of view of ordinary people. "If one-half or even one-quarter of [the trillions of dollars spent on arms during the Cold War] had been intelligently devoted to social and economic progress," a UN report concluded, "then it may be reasonably assumed that we could now be living in a world in which mass hunger, malnutrition, preventable disease, illiteracy, rapid population growth and a deteriorating global environment would be problems of the past."

Obscene amounts of money are spent every year on the means to kill larger and larger numbers of people more effectively. And why? Because capitalism's blind drive for profit produces not only economic devastation but military conflicts between different groups of national rulers. The drive to war is built into the system.

Looming over any talk of war in the 21st century is the threat of nuclear annihilation—a war fought with weapons that could destroy the basis of all life on the planet. But this nightmare isn't even limited to war. The everyday workings of the capitalist system wreak havoc on the environment.

For example, by the end of the 1990s, a growing number of studies were confirming that pollution from the burning of fossil fuels like coal and oil was leading to a small but significant increase in global temperatures. Scientists had been warning for years before that "global warming" of even a few degrees would upset a delicate natural balance and have catastrophic consequences—widespread flooding, the spread of tropical diseases, terrible draughts, more severe weather conditions.

Any rational society would have long ago taken steps to stop the so-called "greenhouse" effect. But international treaties designed to reduce emissions of greenhouse gases are drops in the bucket—and even these have met opposition from U.S. bosses. The sick truth is that it's profitable to pollute—even if that means destruction of the environment on a vast and irreversible scale.

This is the madness of the free market. Capitalism does one thing very well—protect and increase the wealth of the people at the top of society. Meeting the needs of everyone else is secondary, which is why so many people's needs go unmet. From every other point of view—producing enough to go around, protecting the environment, building a society of equality and freedom—the capitalist system is entirely irrational.

From Good Times to Hard Times

Nothing exposes the madness of capitalism more clearly—and with more terrible consequences for huge numbers of people—than the regular economic upheavals that plague the free-market system.

At the beginning of 1999, half the world was in the grip of an economic crisis. It began a little more than a year earlier in Asia—among the very countries long held up as examples of how capitalism was supposed to work. Throughout the decade before, the so-called Pacific Tiger economies of Southeast Asia grew rapidly. The biggest of them, South Korea, became a significant industrial power. In Indonesia, millions of peasants and rural laborers were drawn into the cities to look for jobs in the new factories.

Then, suddenly, the Asian boom was over. Beginning in the summer of 1997, a panic spread from one country to another. Turmoil on the financial markets led to huge price increases for basic products such as rice and cooking oil. In South Korea, tens of thousands of workers whose labor had transformed the country found themselves kicked out in the street. In Indonesia, laid-off workers fled back to the countryside in the hopes of finding a way to scrape out a living for themselves and their families.

What happened? The economic commentators who before were so smug and confident about the Tigers' future looked for scapegoats—often among the Asian bosses they praised in preceding years. But mostly they were baffled.

This isn't unusual. Political and business leaders who take credit for the economic good times are quick to throw up their hands in a crisis. We're encouraged to think that economic slumps are just part of the way of things. In his novel about the auto industry, *The Fliver King,* the American writer Upton Sinclair described "people losing their jobs, and not being able to find others; it was something known as hard times; a natural phenomenon like winter itself, mysterious, universal, cruel."

But there's nothing "natural" or "mysterious" about capitalism's economic crises. They are the direct result of the drive for more profits.

At the heart of the Asian crisis—and the worldwide recession that crept toward the U.S.—is what Karl Marx and Frederick Engels called a "crisis of overproduction." Marx and Engels argued that the headlong expansion of capitalism during economic good times laid the basis for slumps to come—because capitalists eventually produce more products than they can sell at a decent profit. When profits fall, the bosses rush to cut costs—and that means cutting back on investments, laying off workers and closing factories.

As Marx and Engels wrote in the *Communist Manifesto:*

> In these crises there breaks out an epidemic that, in all earlier epochs, would have seemed an absurdity—the epidemic of overproduction. Society suddenly finds it-

self put back into a state of momentary barbarism; it appears as if a famine, a universal war of devastation had cut off the supply of every means of subsistence; industry and commerce seem to be destroyed. And why? Because there is too much civilization, too much means of subsistence, too much industry, too much commerce.

The 150-year-old *Communist Manifesto* could have been written yesterday about the Asian crisis. The secret to the stunning growth of the "Tigers" was a huge boom in producing goods for sale around the world. But as more and more countries joined in, trying to copy the Tiger model, the world became glutted with more products than could be sold at a decent profit. Banks and international investors which fueled Asia's boom with big loans to the Tigers pulled their money out when the stream of profits slowed down—setting off the financial panics that ushered in the crisis.

The problem of "overproduction" isn't confined to Asia. "What imperils the world economy most?" the *Wall Street Journal* asked in a 1998 article. "Everything—or, rather, too much of everything. From cashmere to blue jeans, silver jewelry to aluminum cans, the world is in oversupply."

Of course, there's a crying need around the world for all of the goods supposedly "in oversupply." But because of the sick logic of the system, when bosses can't make a profit selling their products, they go to waste. Even the *Wall Street Journal*—never anything other than a mouthpiece for the bosses—had to admit that "a moral dimension shadows the very notion of overcapacity when billions of people live in poverty, deprived of many of the goods and services that saturate the developed world."

Food rots while people around the world go hungry. Shut-down steel mills rust as millions live without homes.

Computer factories close while schools—even in the U.S., the richest country in the world—lack the latest technology they need to teach students effectively. This is the reality of a system organized around making profits for the privileged few—no matter what the cost in terms of human misery.

The Socialist Answer

Socialism is based on the idea that we should use the vast resources of society to meet people's needs.

It seems so obvious—that if people are hungry, they should be fed; that if people are homeless, we should build homes for them; that if people are sick, all the advances in medical technology should be available to them. But capitalism produces the opposite.

A socialist society would take the vast wealth of the rich and use it to meet the basic needs of all society. We'll take all the money wasted on weapons and use it to end poverty and homelessness and all other forms of scarcity. We'll abolish advertising and make sure that everyone can get a good education.

There's no blueprint for what a socialist society will look like—that will be determined by the generations to come who live in one. But it seems obvious that such a society would begin by guaranteeing that every family has enough to eat and a sturdy roof over their head. The education system would be made free—and reorganized so that every child's ability is encouraged. Health care would immediately be made free and accessible, as would all utilities like gas and electricity. So would public transportation—and a far better funded and more efficient system it would be. All these basic needs would become top priorities.

A socialist society would not only take away the existing wealth of the ruling class but also its economic control over the world. The means of production—the factories and offices and mines and so on—would be owned by all of society. Rather than important economic decisions being left to the chaos of the free market and the blind competition of capitalists scrambling to make a profit, under socialism, the majority would plan what to do democratically.

Not surprisingly, such ideas bring loud complaints from defenders of the capitalist system. Most come down to the same thing—that public ownership and planning would involve a bunch of bureaucrats ordering people around and telling them what they should want.

That's pretty ridiculous coming from supporters of the current system. Under capitalism, most people have no meaningful choice about anything that really matters in their lives—what they do at work and how they do it, what they can buy, how they spend the bulk of their time. These decisions are made in the corporate boardrooms, in the Oval Office, in the judges' chambers—without anyone being consulted.

The idea of socialist planning is based on the exact opposite of this—the widest possible debate and discussion about what's needed in society and how to achieve it. Instead of leaving decisions about what gets produced and how to a handful of executives, all workers would have a voice in what they do at their workplace. And larger bodies of democratically elected representatives would be able to have a full discussion of overall social priorities.

If a socialist society by mistake produced too much of one kind of product, we could give away the extra and shift resources to making something else. When capitalists make this kind of mistake, factories are shut down, workers are thrown out on the street, food is destroyed to push up prices and so on. Socialism would put an end to this absurd waste.

For planning to work, a socialist society must be democratic—much more democratic than the current system. Democracy and capitalism don't really go hand in hand. In fact, many of the models of the free market in the less developed world are run by repressive dictatorships. Even in societies that brag about being democratic, democracy is limited to electing our representatives to government every two or four years.

Socialism will be democratic in a more fundamental way. Unfortunately, the record of the former USSR, China and other so-called socialist countries has left the impression that socialism is a top-down society run by party bosses. This has nothing to do with genuine socialism—or, for that matter, the whole experience of working-class struggle.

There have been many revolutionary upheavals during the 20th century—from the 1917 revolution in Russia to Spain's revolution in the 1930s to the Iranian revolution of 1979, to mention only a few examples. And each one has created a similar system for the majority in society to make decisions about how to organize the struggle and what priorities to set. Each time, democracy revolved around a system of workers' councils. These are representative bodies elected from workplaces—because the production of wealth in society takes place at work, making the workplace a better basis for a system that controls how to use that wealth.

All the different examples of workers' councils over the

years have shared common features—of immediate recall so workers can control those they elect; of not paying representatives more than the people they represent or allowing them to rise above anyone else's social level; of elections taking place at mass meetings rather than in the isolation of the voting booth.

The exact shape of workers' councils in a future socialist society can't be predicted. But what's important is the democratic principle that these bodies have represented in past struggles. The basic principle common to all revolutions is that representatives have to be held accountable to the people they represent. This can only be accomplished if discussion and argument thrives in every corner of society—and if representatives are responsible to the outcomes of the discussions. Such a system would be many times more democratic than what exists in today's world.

The heart of socialism is making equality a reality. Marx and Engels summed up this aim with a simple slogan: "From each according to their ability, to each according to their need."

This basic concept infuriates the bosses and their ideologues. They simply can't grasp the idea of a society without power and privilege for a small group of people. They complain that under socialism, everyone would be paid the same. This is true. Roughly speaking, people would receive the same thing—there's no reason for it to work any other way. "Ah ha," comes the response. "You'd pay a brain surgeon the same as you pay a garbageman. Then no one would become brain surgeons, and everyone would become garbagemen."

Think about what a statement like that says about the priorities of capitalist society. It says that the only reason people do the exacting work of trying to heal sick people is for money. Without a financial incentive, everyone would be happy with the thankless and certainly unfulfilling job of picking up garbage.

What a travesty. Socialism would be about giving people the opportunity to do what they really want to do—allow them to become doctors or scientists or artists or anything else they desire. We would use our technological knowledge to eliminate boring jobs like collecting garbage as much as possible—and share out equally the tasks we couldn't. The goal would be to free all people to do the work they love—and to give them the leisure time to enjoy all the wonders of the world around them.

Capitalism stifles people's creativity. Only a minority are asked to put their minds to thinking about society—and most of them do it for the purpose of making themselves richer, not for achieving any common good.

Imagine a society in which it mattered what ordinary people thought about what they were doing—where it mattered what an assembly-line worker thought about the pace of work and whether it was necessary, what a hospital worker thought about the availability of medical resources and how they should be used. That's a world in which people would become fully alive in a way they never will under capitalism.

Can the System Be Fixed?

The basic idea of socialism—that the resources of society should be used to meet people's needs—seems like the simplest of proposals. The more difficult question is how to achieve it. How can society be transformed?

In high school civics class, the textbooks talked about political change taking place "through the system." The U.S. government represents the "will of the people," we were taught. People who want to "make a difference" should use the democratic process—by working for political candidates they like and maybe even running for office themselves.

But to judge from Election 2000, the chances of "making a difference" aren't too good.

The main qualification for becoming a serious candidate for president, for example, had nothing to do with "political vision" or any of the overblown phrases thrown around in the media. It was the ability to raise outrageous sums of money from wealthy donors. George W. Bush got the jump on the other candidates. By the beginning of 2000—almost a year before the election—Bush had raked in $67 million, already three times the previous record set by Bill Clinton during his 1996 campaign.

Some of the same politicians who pocketed big bucks from Corporate America complained about the influence of money on elections. But that's what makes the U.S. political system tick. Money rules. From the presidential race on down, our "choice" in the important contests of Election 2000 was all but decided by a special class of voters—the millionaires voting with their checkbooks.

Of course, winning an election also means getting ordinary people to vote for you. All the candidates—even the most dyed-in-the-wool Republican toadies for big business— talk about "serving the people" and giving ordinary Americans a better deal. But this is a fraud—a fraud that reflects the basic nature of government under capitalism. The politicians are the public face of a system that's set up to serve the rich. Their job is to say one thing to the majority of people to win their votes—while doing another for their real masters.

Broken promises are par for the course—and the presidency of Bill Clinton is a prime example. It takes a real effort to remember that millions of people looked forward to the 1992 elections with a sense of hope. After 12 years of Republicans in the White House, baldly attacking workers and the poor, Bill Clinton was promising "change." He was going to fix the U.S. economy, then in the grips of a recession. He was going to reform the broken-down health-care system. He was going to "put people first" after years of the Republicans' mean-spirited scapegoating.

But Clinton hadn't even entered the Oval Office before he began breaking promises—starting with pledges to end discrimination against gays and lesbians in the military and to grant asylum to Haitian refugees locked up at the U.S. naval base at Guantanamo Bay, Cuba. Other parts of the agenda disappeared within a few months. Clinton didn't lift a finger as legislation to ban the use of scabs during strikes went down to defeat in the Senate—controlled at the time by the Democrats.

Clinton took a full two years to screw up health-care reform. With his wife Hillary Rodham Clinton leading the way, Clinton compromised away one provision after another in the hope of staying on the good side of the health-care bosses. The final proposal was such a mess that congressional Republicans succeeded in portraying it as "big-government liberalism" run amok. Health-care reform—the centerpiece of Clinton's 1992 campaign—never even came to a vote in Congress.

After two years of disillusionment, Clinton voters stayed home for the 1994 congressional election. The Democrats were routed, ushering in the so-called "Republican Revolution." House Speaker Newt Gingrich took charge in Congress. He talked a lot about a "political sea change"—that the U.S. public had finally come around to the Republican way.

But the 1994 elections were a vote against Clinton, not a vote for the Republicans. As Gingrich steadily became the most hated man in U.S. politics, Clinton was able to make a comeback. But he didn't do it by challenging the Republican attack. Instead, he stole the Republican program and offered a gentler version of it.

The legislation that Clinton signed into law in the years that followed was more than Ronald Reagan or George Bush could have dreamed of. In 1995, Clinton agreed to a proposal to balance the federal budget that required across-the-board spending cuts. Departments like the Occupational Safety and Health Administration and the Environmental Protection Agency suffered the consequences. And the next year,

Clinton signed the Republicans' version of welfare "reform."

The GOP was furious. "The good news is that we're going to have a Republican president in 1996," snarled one disgruntled Republican. "The bad news is that it will be Bill Clinton."

Clinton did win reelection in 1996—thanks to the continuing hatred for Republicans. But rather than go on the offensive, Clinton promised to pursue bipartisanship—a code word for more Lite versions of Republican proposals. Within the year, he had agreed to a cut in the capital gains tax—an appalling giveaway to the rich. Reagan's crackpot economic advisers first proposed the capital gains tax cut in the 1980s, but it was Clinton who finally delivered.

In 1998, Clinton became only the second president in history to be impeached by the House of Representatives. But at almost every stage in the White House sex scandal, Clinton's approval ratings climbed higher—with a steady majority in opinion polls recognizing impeachment for the slimy maneuver it was. In defending himself, Clinton won support by demanding that Washington focus on the "real issues." But once again, Clinton didn't deliver. Proposals around child care and education—floated to divert attention—were quietly dropped by an administration that didn't really care about them in the first place. They joined a trail of broken promises that led back to the day Clinton was elected president.

Do the Democrats Make a Difference?

Politicians like Bill Clinton are a dime a dozen. The only characteristic that distinguishes Clinton is that he's better than most at the most important skill for a politician—talking out of both sides of his mouth.

There's a reason why people consider used-car dealers

to be more trustworthy than politicians. Politicians claim they're answerable to "the people." But they're really answerable to the bosses who control U.S. society. President Woodrow Wilson admitted as much at the beginning of the 20th century:

> Suppose you go to Washington and try to get at your government. You will always find that while you are politely listened to, the men really consulted are the men who have the big stake—the big bankers, the big manufacturers and the big masters of commerce... The masters of the government of the United States are the combined capitalists and manufacturers of the United States.

Nearly a century later, Wilson's words ring as true as ever. Both of the main political parties in the U.S. are run in the interests of those who control the purse strings— and they, overwhelmingly, are the bosses. As Mel Sembler, finance chair for the Republican National Committee, put it after a meeting with the party's "Team 100"—people who donated more than $100,000: "These are our investors, these are our stockholders."

Republicans have always done better than Democrats at coming up with money from rich donors. But the Democrats regularly rake in big bucks from corporations. And there are plenty of players who give money to both sides. During the 1992 election, Atlantic Richfield, Archer Daniels Midland, RJR Nabisco, Philip Morris and the Tobacco Institute all gave more than $100,000 to both parties.

It's obvious why money plays such an important role— Washington politics is about money. During the 1998 election campaign, contributions to the major parties hit a record $1.6 billion. Business gave 63 percent of the cash— compared to less than 3 percent from unions, which are regularly denounced by Republicans for trying to control Washington. And despite the deluge of cash, voter turnout dropped to the lowest point in more than half a century.

Big business doesn't give away all that money for the hell of it. They expect something in return. A few years ago, Republican House leaders were caught allowing business lobbyists to actually write the legislation that gutted environmental regulations. But if most politicians aren't so brazen, this is basically how it's done in Washington.

All this explains why both Republicans and Democrats regularly do the bidding of the bosses—that's who contributes money to their campaigns. Of course, Republicans and Democrats aren't exactly alike. On any given issue, most Republicans are likely to be more conservative than most Democrats. But the differences between the two parties are minor in comparison to the fundamental similarities that unite them.

Nevertheless, the differences are important in terms of how the two parties are seen by most people. It's been many years since anyone thought of the Republicans as anything other than the party of big business. But the Democrats have the reputation of being the party of the people—the mainstream party that looks out for the interests of labor and minorities.

The truth is quite different.

The Democrats' image dates back to the Great Depression of the 1930s and President Franklin Delano Roosevelt's New Deal reforms, which laid the basis for many of the programs we associate with the federal government today—like Social Security and unemployment insurance, for example. These were important victories, and it's no wonder that workers look back on the politicians associated with them as friends of labor.

But that's not what Roosevelt thought of himself. "[T]hose who have property [fail] to realize that I am the best friend the profit system ever had," Roosevelt said. In fact, Roosevelt carried out the New Deal reforms as a conscious effort to head off a social revolt sparked by the Great Depression. In return, he got labor's votes—cementing the labor movement's misplaced loyalty to the Democrats that lasts to this day.

The Democrats played much the same role during the social upheavals of the 1960s. Presidents John F. Kennedy and Lyndon Johnson today have an entirely unearned reputation as anti-racists because they eventually supported some civil rights reforms. But they had to be dragged into it. Kennedy did his best to ignore the growing civil rights movement in the U.S. South. And it was only after the Black struggle grew to explosive proportions that Johnson—a southern Democrat with a long record of opposing civil rights—pushed through the Civil Rights Act of 1964 and the Voting Rights Act of 1965, the two key pieces of 1960s civil rights legislation.

The Democrats succeeded in co-opting a number of leaders of social movements, eventually putting them into the position of managing the system. For example, in the late 1960s, the Democratic Party—once the party of Southern slavery—opened its doors to Black politicians. The number of Black officeholders shot up to more than 10,000 elected officials. Most major U.S. cities have had an African American mayor for some period of time. But these politicians—elected with the hope that they would challenge racism—have carried out the same attacks. They've ended up imposing the cuts in social services and defending racist police.

But in spite of their record, at every election, the Democrats have been able to count on their reputation as champions of workers and the poor. Consider the fact that Bill Clinton—after all of his broken promises—has had the uninterrupted support of organized labor and liberal organizations. In fact, these groups at various times disarmed opposition to Clinton's policies. On the eve of Clinton's signing of welfare "reform" legislation in August 1996, Marian Wright Edelman, head of the Children's Defense Fund, called off a planned demonstration in Washington, D.C., at the urging of the White House.

In fact, the bosses got away with welfare "reform" without much of a fight at all. That's because the liberal organizations that could have organized a response insisted it was more important to stand behind Clinton for fear of getting something worse—a Republican victory in the 1996 election.

This is a perfect example of the politics of "lesser evilism." The argument—which emerges at every election—is that people should hold their nose and vote for Democrats as the lesser evil in order to avoid the greater evil of a Republican victory.

The problem is that in voting for the lesser evil, you usually get the lesser and the greater evil. That's because politicians like Clinton won't make any concessions to our side if they know we're in their back pocket. If Clinton thinks he can take the support of liberal organizations for granted, then he'll sign laws like welfare "reform" without a second thought—on the assumption that he can win a few more votes by appealing to the right.

That's why we need an independent alternative to the twin parties of capitalism.

The Limits of Reform

Not every country that calls itself a democracy is dominated by two political parties that stand for capitalism.

Most countries of Western Europe have mass parties associated with the labor movement—and by the late 1990s, these parties were running the governments in France, Germany, Britain and elsewhere.

So would we come closer to socialism in the U.S. if we could vote for a political party that stood for the working class rather than the capitalist class? This would certainly be an advance over what exists now——if elections offered workers the chance to vote for a labor party. But ultimately, socialism can't come through the ballot box.

We're encouraged to believe that government stands above society—that it's the negotiator between competing groups like employers and workers. But this is an illusion. Governments in capitalist societies are tools of the ruling class. One reason for this has already been shown—that the bosses have a lot bigger say in what our elected representatives decide to do. But there's more to the question.

Governments consist of much more than elected representatives. There are the unelected bureaucracies that make crucial decisions affecting people's lives—decisions made by people who aren't answerable in any way to the rest of society. Then there's the judicial side of the U.S. government. Federal judges all the way up to the Supreme Court never face an election. And standing beyond all this are what Frederick Engels called "bodies of armed men"—the police and the army. Formally, the Pentagon may be answerable to elected politicians. But in reality, it's a power unto itself.

Because of this, even politicians with every intention of "making a difference" find that rather than being able to pull the levers of power, the levers of power pull them. They end up managing the system they expected to change.

Suppose you were elected president and were determined to impose a tax on the rich to pay for a system of universal health care. Within minutes of taking office, you would get a visit from your Treasury Secretary, who at least you had appointed, and the chair of the government's central bank, the Federal Reserve, who you didn't have any say about. They would tell you that Wall Street wanted nothing to do with your plan unless you compromised. If you persisted, the bosses would take further action—sending their money out of the country so it couldn't be taxed and causing turbulence on the financial markets until you said "uncle."

The "realistic" response is to make concessions—to try to find some arrangement that's acceptable to all sides. But when this becomes the priority, politics turns into the art of compromise rather than a campaign to accomplish something. And that shapes the plans and outlook of the people trying to make change in a system rigged against them.

But beyond all these considerations, the fact is that many of the most important decisions about people's lives have nothing to do with decisions made by elected officials. For example, no politician voted for the tens of thousands of layoffs at AT&T. The only people who had a say in that decision were AT&T executives—answerable, if at all, to the tiny handful of people rich enough to own a significant chunk of the company's stock.

This is why the system can't be reformed. Elected representatives are only one part of government under capitalism. And in a number of tragic examples in countries around the world, they've turned out to be a dispensable part—when sections of the ruling class decided to ditch democracy and rule by brute force.

The most famous case of this comes from Chile. The socialist Salvador Allende was elected president in 1970 on a fairly mild program of reform that included nationalizing parts of the economy. Many people took this as a sign that socialism could be elected into power. But for the next three years, Chile's bosses—and their international partners, especially in the U.S.—did everything they could to sabotage Allende. They succeeded in forcing him to compromise. But compromise wasn't good enough. When the time was ripe, Chile's generals made their move—launching a bloody coup that claimed the lives of tens of thousands of Chilean workers.

The truth is that, even if they weren't bought off, politicians don't have the power to make the kind of change that would really transform society. Instead of trying to get well-intentioned politicians elected to make what changes they can, we need to overturn the whole system.

That is what a revolution is all about. It is about taking away the power of the people at the top of society to make unaccountable decisions that affect our lives. It is about getting rid of a state machine organized to preserve the system as it exists. And it is about organizing a completely different and more democratic system of workers' councils to make decisions about society.

This doesn't mean that socialists don't care about reforms. In fact, outside of revolutionary upheavals, socialists spend most of their efforts mobilizing pressure to win changes in the existing system. Reforms make workers lives easier and increase their power in the here and now. And they make people more confident in the struggle to win further change. As the revolutionary Rosa Luxemburg wrote:

> Can we counterpose the social revolution, the transformation of the existing social order, our final goal, to social reforms? Certainly not. The daily struggle for reforms, for the amelioration of the condition of the workers within the framework of the existing social order, and for democratic institutions, offers to [socialists] the only means of engaging in the proletarian

class war and working in the direction of the final goal—the conquest of political power and the suppression of wage labor. Between social reforms and revolution there exists…an indissoluble tie. The struggle for reforms is its means; the social revolution, its aim.

Socialists fight for reforms. But reforms by themselves aren't enough—because they can be taken back if the movement retreats. We need revolution because capitalist society can't be permanently changed in any other way.

"If There Is No Struggle, There Is No Progress"

When socialists talk about the need for a revolution to fundamentally change society, we're often accused of being unrealistic and utopian. The argument starts in different ways—people are bought off by the system, they're made stupid by television and popular culture, the U.S. government itself is so powerful that it can't be challenged. But it always ends with the question: How can a revolution ever take place in the U.S.?

Actually, the question isn't *whether* a revolution can take place in the U.S. The question is whether *another* revolution can take place.

In a little more than two centuries, the U.S. has had two revolutions. The first, in 1776, overthrew colonial rule by Britain's monarchy. That struggle spread to every corner of society and produced a new nation organized around a representative government and perhaps the widest system of democracy known to the world to that point. There were gaping holes—the terrible crime of slavery was left untouched, for example. But the new United States was an advance over what came before.

The U.S. experienced another social revolution 90 years later—the Civil War of 1861-65, which destroyed the Southern system of slavery. Today, credit for "freeing the slaves" usually goes to Abraham Lincoln and perhaps a few army generals. But the North would never have won the war against slavery without the active participation of masses of people. Black slaves themselves played a crucial role in sparking the struggle, as did the agitators of the abolitionist movement in the North. And it was the soldiers in the Northern army—many of whom started without a clear idea of the war's aim but were convinced over time of the need to abolish slavery—whose courage and sacrifice transformed U.S. society.

The War of 1776 and the Civil War weren't socialist revolutions. They were revolutions against national oppression and slavery that left the economic setup of capitalism intact. Nevertheless, these struggles fundamentally shaped U.S. society—and they disprove the picture of a country that's always been stable and quiet.

What's more, the years since have produced other uprisings that shook U.S. society to its foundations—the struggle for the eight-hour day during the 1880s; the "great red year" of 1919, when one in five U.S. workers was on strike; the 1930s movements, including the battle to win mass unionization; and the 1960s, which opened with the civil rights movement in the South and closed with struggles that questioned everything about U.S. society, from the brutal war in Vietnam to the oppression of women and gays and lesbians.

This way of looking at the past is very different from what passes for history in school. To begin with, the way history is usually taught—remembering the names of famous people and the dates when they did something important—is upside down. The course of history depends, first and foremost, not on what a few "great men" did or thought but on the struggles of huge numbers of people, especially during the times when they organized themselves in rebellions and revolutions. It's not that figures like George Washington and Abraham Lincoln are unimportant. But what they did and what they're remembered for today was shaped by the actions of masses of people who aren't remembered at all.

Bertolt Brecht made this point in a poem called "Questions from a Worker Who Reads":

> Who built Thebes of the seven gates?
> In the books you will find the names of kings.
> Did the kings haul up the lumps of rock?
> And Babylon, many times demolished
> Who raised it up so many times? In what houses
> Of gold-glittering Lima did the builders live?
> Where, the evening that the Wall of China was finished
> Did the masons go?…
>
> The young Alexander conquered India.
> Was he alone?
> Caesar beat the Gauls.
> Did he not have even a cook with him?
> Philip of Spain wept when his armada
> Went down. Was he the only one to weep?
> Frederick the Second won the Seven Years' War. Who
> Else won it?
>
> Every page a victory.
> Who cooked the feast for the victors?
> Every ten years a great man.
> Who paid the bill?

Something else flows from a socialist view of history. We're encouraged to believe that political and social change—if it happens at all—takes place at a safe, gradual pace. Let any group of people organize to show their opposition to an injustice, and they're certain to be told to be patient—to let the system work as it has in the past. But this goes against the whole history of the struggle for justice and equality. For example, in the first half of the 19th century, virtually every U.S. politician, North and South, believed that the enslavement of Blacks would die out eventually if the Southern slave system was left alone. Yet the slave power only grew. It took a civil war to put an end to this horror.

The U.S. is supposed to be the most stable of countries. But revolutions and social upheavals are a constant theme. And most of the reforms that workers take for granted today are a product of those upheavals. For example, unemployment insurance was introduced as part of President Franklin Delano Roosevelt's New Deal program of the 1930s. Roosevelt didn't come up with the idea. He was forced by the crisis of the Great Depression and by massive social pressure to adopt an idea put forward by workers.

Of course, political leaders like Roosevelt always end up with the credit in the history books for the reforms they were forced to carry out. But this doesn't change the fact that they were *forced* to act—regardless of their political affiliation. Consider this: Republican President Richard Nixon launched more anti-discrimination and affirmative action programs than Democratic President Bill Clinton. That's not because Nixon was more liberal—on the contrary, he was a miserable right winger. But Nixon was under pressure to act from the mass social movements of the 1960s and early 1970s—something Clinton hasn't faced.

The great abolitionist leader Frederick Douglass made all this plain with these words:

> The whole history of the progress of human liberty
> shows that all concessions yet made to her august

claims have been born of earnest struggle…If there is no struggle, there is no progress. Those who profess to favor freedom and yet deprecate agitation are men who want crops without plowing up the ground, they want rain without thunder and lightning. They want the ocean without the awful roar of its mighty waters. The struggle may be a moral one, or it may be a physical one, and it may be both moral and physical, but it must be a struggle. Power concedes nothing without a demand. It never did and it never will.

A Power Greater Than Their Hoarded Gold

For hundreds if not thousands of years, most societies around the world have been divided between exploiters and exploited—between a ruling class of people that runs society in its own interest and much larger exploited classes whose labor is the source of their rulers' wealth and power. Under each system, the biggest conflicts have been between these classes—over who rules, who gets ruled over and how. As Karl Marx and Frederick Engels put it in the *Communist Manifesto:*

> The history of all hitherto existing society is the history of class struggles. Freeman and slave, patrician and plebeian, lord and serf, guildmaster and journeyman, in a word, oppressor and oppressed, stood in constant opposition to one another, carried on an uninterrupted, now hidden, now open fight…

In all these societies, the oppressed have dreamed of a future world of equality and justice where their oppression would end. And they have fought for it—from the slave rebellion against the Roman Empire led by Spartacus to the peasant uprisings in Europe, among others.

So the ideals of socialism aren't new. But the possibility of achieving them is the product of only the last few centuries—in most parts of the world, of just the last 100 years.

Why? Because socialism can't be organized on the basis of scarcity. Unless there's enough to go around, there's certain to be a scramble over who gets what. That scramble is bound to produce a class society—a society in which one group of people organizes the system to make sure they get enough, even if others go without. Only under the system of capitalism has human knowledge and technology been raised to the point where we can feed every person on the planet, cloth them, put a roof over their head and so on.

So under capitalism, there's no longer any natural reason for poverty to exist. But abolishing poverty means getting rid of a system that causes it—and that requires a social force capable of overthrowing it. Marx and Engels argued that, in the process of its development, capitalism produced "its own gravediggers"—the working class, with the power to overthrow the system and establish a new society not divided between rulers and ruled.

Why did Marx and Engels talk about the working class? Not because workers suffer the most under capitalism or because they're morally superior to any other group. Socialists focus on the position that workers occupy in the capitalist economy. Their labor produces the profits that make the system tick. The working class as a whole has a special power to paralyze the system—to bring the profit system to a halt by not working.

You can see this power in situations that fall well short of revolution. In March 1996, General Motors provoked a strike of 3,200 autoworkers at two Dayton, Ohio, factories that made brake parts for most GM vehicles. It was a huge blunder. Within a week, the walkout had crippled GM's production across North America. All but two of the company's assembly plants had to close down. GM lost about $1 billion in profits in 15 days. Management gave in.

By the same token, a *general* strike by workers throughout the economy can paralyze a whole country—and bring a government to its knees. That's what happened in Poland in 1980 with the revolt of the Solidarnosc trade union. The upheaval began with a strike by shipyard workers in Gdansk, but it soon spread to involve 10 million workers across the country. Within weeks, democratically organized workers' committees sprang up to organize the strike and to make decisions about how to provide essential services. The so-called "socialist" government—a dictatorial regime with a long record of vicious repression—was powerless to restore order for more than a year. Before the strike, Polish workers would never have guessed that they could rock a seemingly all-powerful police state. But they cut off the lifeblood of the system—the wealth they created by their labor.

Of course, other groups in capitalist society can and do fight back. For example, during the 1960s, the biggest upheavals in the U.S. involved African Americans fighting for civil rights and against racism. These were magnificent struggles that won real and lasting changes. And they inspired other parts of society to fight. But by themselves, Blacks didn't have the power to transform the whole system. First, they were a minority of the population. And organized as a community, African Americans had the moral power to embarrass and persuade—but not the kind of economic power to hit the bosses where it hurts.

Struggles organized on the basis of class have the potential of uniting the working majority in society. They hold out the promise of overcoming divisions among the have-nots—and uniting people to fight on a common basis, not only for the demands they have in common but for the special demands of specific groups. And what's more, workers' struggles represent a direct threat to our rulers' wealth—to the source of their power over society.

But workers only have power if they're united. "Labor in white skin cannot emancipate itself where it is branded in Black skin," Marx wrote about slavery in the U.S. His point can be extended to every form of bigotry and discrimination. That's why it's crucial for socialists to champion all fights against oppression. These struggles are just in their own right. But they're also critical in building working-class unity.

Unity has to be fought for. But there's something about the nature of work under capitalism that pushes workers to fight—and to organize that fight in a collective way.

First of all, the whole dynamic of capitalism is for the bosses to try to increase their wealth by squeezing more profits out of workers. That means trying to get workers to work harder for the same or less pay. This drive for profit puts the bosses on a collision course with workers.

Moreover, capitalism forces workers to cooperate with one another at work—and that goes for resistance as well. Individuals can stand up for their rights at work, but only to a certain point. It's too easy to get rid of troublemakers if they stand alone. Solidarity is necessary to win the bigger fights.

That's even more true as struggles progress. Because capitalism brings workers together in large numbers, it's easier for workers to discuss and debate the way forward and to make collective decisions about what needs to be done. And the cooperative arrangements of work lay the basis for organizing a future society based on collective control. Workers can't divide up a workplace—with one taking the drill press, the other a computer terminal, another a Xerox machine. They have to work together to make use of the resources around them.

"Solidarity forever" and "An injury to one is an injury to all" are old slogans of the labor movement. But they're more than good ideas. They are absolutely necessary for workers to win.

When Marx and Engels were writing in the middle of the 19th century, the working class was tiny—perhaps 2 or 3 million people, concentrated in Britain, a few countries in northwestern Europe and along the northeastern coast of the U.S. Today, there are more workers in South Korea than there were around the world in Marx and Engels' time.

Everywhere across the globe, people's lives are shaped by the fact that they have to work for a boss to survive. But the flip side of this reality is that workers have enormous power. And they have shown that power in struggles in every corner of the world. The final words of Marx and Engels' *Communist Manifesto* are more relevant today than ever before: "The proletarians have nothing to lose but their chains. They have a world to win."

Can Workers Change Society?

If we were to judge only from what we see around us, it might be hard to have confidence that the majority of people can organize to win fundamental change. After all, most working people aren't revolutionaries. Most of the time, they accept a number of ideas that justify the status quo— from the old cliché that you can't fight city hall to the belief that people at the top of society are somehow specially qualified to run it.

This is partly because we're continually exposed to different institutions that are in the business of reinforcing these prejudices. The mass media are one example. Watch the local television news, and you'll see sensationalized stories about crime and violence—while discussion about the real issues that affect people's lives get shortchanged. The poor are stereotyped and scapegoated, while the wealth and power of the rich are celebrated. Even shows meant as entertainment tend to reinforce the conventional wisdom.

Likewise, it's easy to see how the education system encourages conformity. Except for the minority of students being trained to rule society, the experience of school is usually alienating. Students are taught to compete against each other—and ultimately to accept the conditions they see around them.

With all the selfish and mean-spirited ideas actively promoted by these voices of authority, it's a wonder that any sense of solidarity survives under capitalism. But it plainly does. This is most obvious in the outpourings of charity in cases of social crisis, like a famine or an earthquake—even when they take place halfway around the world. The kindness and generosity of ordinary people is boundless. But even on a day-to-day basis, society simply couldn't function without a basic sense of cooperation and sacrifice among ordinary people—within families, among coworkers and so on.

The point is that capitalist society obscures this basic decency—because the system is organized around greed. Obviously, those in charge get ahead by being as greedy as possible. But working people are forced—whether they like it or not—to participate in a rat race that they have no control over. They're pitted against one another and required to compete just to keep their job or maintain their standard of living—much less get ahead.

As a result, the idea of people uniting for social change can seem distant and unrealistic. For most people, the experience of their lives teaches them that they don't have any power over what happens in the world—and that they don't know enough to have an opinion about it anyway. Powerlessness produces what appears to be apathy among people—about their own future and the future of society.

This is why it isn't enough for socialists to talk about why socialism will make an excellent alternative to capitalism. It's also necessary to talk about the struggle to get there—because struggle transforms people and gives them confidence in their own power. As Karl Marx put it, "Revolution is necessary not only because the ruling class cannot be overthrown in any other way but also because the class overthrowing it can only in a revolution succeed in ridding itself of all the muck of ages and become fit to found society anew."

The act of fighting back is the first step in challenging the prejudices learned from living in the dog-eat-dog world of capitalism. This can be seen in even the smallest strike. Strikes almost always start over a specific workplace issue—the demand for higher wages or better conditions. But whatever the original grievance, striking workers who may have thought of themselves as law-abiding citizens are acting in a way that goes against what society teaches them.

Fighting back also requires unity. So striking workers are often forced to question the divisions built up in their ranks—between Black and white, between men and women, between native born and immigrant. As the strike goes on, feelings of solidarity and a sense of the wider issues at stake start to become as important as the original issues.

The changes that take place are profound. Take the "War Zone" labor struggles in Illinois in the mid-1990s. The center of the War Zone was Decatur, Ill., a small industrial city where workers were on strike or locked out at three companies—the food processor A.E. Staley, the heavy equipment manufacturer Caterpillar and tire-maker

Bridgestone-Firestone.

Several months into the struggles, activists organized a multiracial march to celebrate Martin Luther King's birthday—in a town where the Ku Klux Klan had organized, both before and since. The War Zone workers were drawing on King's statements about the fight for civil rights to explain what their struggles were about—and to show that they had come to see that their fight for justice in the workplace was linked to other fights in society.

In the course of any struggle, activists committed to the fight around a particular issue have to grapple with questions about their aims—what kind of change they want and how to achieve it. Their answers evolve with their experiences.

Think of the Black college students who joined the civil rights movement in the 1960s. In 1960, one member of the newly formed Student Nonviolent Coordinating Committee could tell a reporter that she was motivated by traditional American values. If only Blacks were given educational opportunities, she said, "maybe someday a Negro will invent one of our [nuclear] missiles." A few years later, many SNCC members considered themselves revolutionaries. They had been through the Freedom Rides to desegregate interstate bus lines, the murder of civil rights workers during the Freedom Summer voter registration project in 1964 and the Democratic Party's betrayal of civil rights delegates at its 1964 national convention. These experiences convinced them that the struggle against racial injustice could only be won by linking it to the fight against other injustices—and for a different kind of society altogether.

This transformation was repeated throughout the 1960s and early 1970s. White college students who volunteered for Freedom Summer used the skills they learned from the civil rights movement to organize the struggle against the U.S. war in Vietnam. Veterans of the antiwar movement in turn launched the struggle for women's rights, including the right to choose abortion. The modern gay and lesbian movement was born in 1969 with the formation of the Gay Liberation Front—an organization named after the liberation army in Vietnam.

Though the media love to dismiss them today, the struggles of the 1960s are proof that ideas can change with enormous speed. In periods of social upheaval, millions upon millions of people who focused their energy on all sorts of things suddenly turn their attention to the question of transforming society. The biggest struggles of all— revolutions that overturn the existing social order—produce the most extraordinary changes in people. What's most striking about the history of revolutions is the way that ordinary people—trained all their lives to be docile and obedient—suddenly find their voice.

The caricature of revolution passed off by many historians is of a small group of heavily armed fanatics seizing control of the government—and running it to enrich themselves. But this has nothing to do with genuine socialism. A socialist revolution can't be carried out by a minority—even a minority that genuinely wants to improve the lives of the majority. That's because the heart of socialism is mass participation. As the Russian revolutionary Leon Trotsky put it:

> The most indubitable feature of a revolution is the direct interference of the masses in historic events. In ordinary times, the state—be it monarchical or democratic—elevates itself above the nation, and history is made by specialists in that line of business—kings, ministers, bureaucrats, parliamentarians, journalists. But at those crucial moments when the old order becomes no longer endurable to the masses, they break

over the barriers excluding them from the political arena, sweep aside their traditional representatives, and create by their own interference the initial groundwork for a new regime…The history of a revolution is for us first of all a history of the forcible entrance of the masses into the realm of rulership over their own destiny.

The right-wing writers who pass judgement on revolutions also tend to focus on the toppling of governments—the armed insurrection to seize political control. But this is only the final act of a revolution. It's the climax of a much longer period of struggle in which the rulers of society face a growing crisis—at the same time as workers become more confident of their own power.

At the beginning of the process, the goals for change can be modest—a few reforms in the way the system operates. But the struggle to change this or that aspect of society raises deeper questions. People begin to see the connections between the struggles they're involved in and other issues—and the nature of the system itself. Each of these struggles gives workers a further sense of their ability to run society for themselves. The act of taking over political power is the final step of a revolution that has already been felt in every workplace, in every neighborhood and in every corner of society.

Ten Days That Shook the World

The Russian Revolution of 1917 remains the only socialist revolution so far to succeed and survive for any length of time. Though the experience of workers' power was brief—a matter of less than 10 years before the revolution was defeated—it offers a glimpse of what socialism will look like.

Because of this, the Russian Revolution has been the subject of countless lies and slanders. Chief among them is the idea that the 1917 revolution was a coup, organized by the master manipulators Lenin and Trotsky. Nothing could be further from the truth.

The seeds of the revolution lie in the mass hatred of Russia's Tsar—and the misery of poverty and war that the Tsar pr sided over. The Russian Revolution began in February 1917 with nearly spontaneous demonstrations to commemorate International Working Women's Day. These spread within days until the capital of Petrograd was paralyzed and the Tsar was toppled.

Far from a coup, the revolution depended on mass action—on thousands of confrontations like the one described by Trotsky in his *History of the Russian Revolution* between a crowd of workers and the Cossacks, the most brutal and feared unit of the Tsar's army:

> The workers at the Erikson, one of the foremost mills in the Vyborg district, after a morning meeting came out on the Sampsonievsky Prospect, a whole mass, 2,500 of them, and in a narrow place ran into the Cossacks. Cutting their way with the breasts of their horses, the officers first charged through the crowd. Behind them, filling the whole width of the Prospect, galloped the Cossacks. Decisive moment! But the horsemen, cautiously, in a long ribbon, rode through the corridor just made by the officers. "Some of them smiled," Kayurov recalls, "and one of them gave the workers a good wink." This wink was not without meaning. The workers were emboldened with a friendly, not hostile, kind of assurance, and slightly infected the Cossacks with it. The one who winked found imitators. In spite of renewed efforts from the officers, the Cossacks, without openly breaking discipline, failed to force the crowd to disperse, but flowed through it in streams. This was repeated three or four times and brought the two sides even closer together. Individual Cossacks began to reply to the workers'

questions and even to enter into momentary conversations with them. Of discipline, there remained but a thin transparent shell that threatened to break through any second. The officers hastened to separate their patrol from the workers, and, abandoning the idea of dispersing them, lined the Cossacks out across the street as a barrier to prevent the demonstrators from getting to the [center of the city]. But even this did not help: Standing stock-still in perfect discipline, the Cossacks did not hinder the workers from "diving" under their horses. The revolution does not choose its paths: it made its first steps toward victory under the belly of a Cossack's horse.

If Lenin and Trotsky and the Bolshevik Party they led ended up as leaders of the new workers' state, it was because they earned that position. The Bolsheviks eventually won a majority of the representatives to the soviets, the workers' councils. At the time, no one with any knowledge of the situation questioned this mass support. As Martov, a prominent opponent of the Bolsheviks, wrote, "Understand, please, what we have before us after all is a victorious uprising of the proletariat—almost the entire proletariat supports Lenin and expects its social liberation from the uprising."

Even the final act of the revolution—the armed insurrection in October, in which workers took power from the capitalist government left behind after the Tsar—was carried out with a minimum of resistance and violence.

The popular character of the Russian Revolution is also clear simply from looking at its initial accomplishments.

The revolution put an end to Russia's participation in the First World War—the terrible carnage that left millions of workers slaughtered in a conflict over which major powers would dominate the globe. Russia's entry into the war had been accompanied by a wave of patriotic frenzy, but masses of Russians came to reject the slaughter being carried out in the name of the Tsar. The soldiers that the Tsar depended on to defend his rule changed sides and joined the revolution—a decisive step in Russia as it has been in all revolutions.

The Russian Revolution also dismantled the Tsar's empire—what Lenin called a "prison-house" of different nations that suffered for years under Tsarist tyranny. These nations were given the unconditional right to self-determination. The Tsar had used the most vicious anti-Semitism to prop up his rule. Yet after the revolution, Jews led the workers' councils in Russia's two biggest cities. Laws outlawing homosexuality were repealed. Abortion was legalized and made available on demand. And the revolution started to remove the age-old burden of "women's work" in the family by organizing socialized child care and communal kitchens and laundries.

But just listing the proclamations doesn't do justice to the reality of workers power. Russia was a society in the process of being remade from the bottom up.

In the factories, workers began to take charge of production, making decisions about what would be made and at what pace. The country's vast peasantry took over the land of the big landowners. In city neighborhoods, people organized all sorts of communal services.

In general, decisions about the whole of society became decisions that the whole of society played a part in making.

Russia became a cauldron of discussion—where the ideas of all were part of a debate about what to do. The memories of socialists who lived through the revolution are dominated by this sense of people's horizons opening up. As Krupskaya, a veteran of the Bolshevik Party and Lenin's wife, described it:

...I drank in the life around me. The streets in those days presented a curious spectacle: everywhere people stood about in knots, arguing heatedly and discussing the latest events. I used to mingle with the crowd and listen. These street meetings were so interesting that it once took me three hours to walk from Shirokaya Street to the Krzesinska Mansion. The house in which we lived overlooked a courtyard, and even here, if you opened the window at night, you could hear a heated dispute. A soldier would be sitting there, and he always had an audience—usually some of the cooks or house-maids from next door, or some young people. An hour after midnight, you could catch snatches of talk—"Bol-sheviks, Mensheviks..." At three in the morning, "Mi-lyukov, Bolsheviks..." At five—still the same street-cor-ner-meeting talk, politics, etc. Petrograd's white nights are always associated in my mind now with those all-night political disputes.

The tragedy is that workers' power survived for only a short time in Russia. In the years that followed 1917, the world's major powers, including the U.S., organized an invasion force that fought alongside the dregs of Tsarist society—ex-generals, aristocrats and assorted hangers-on—in a civil war against the new workers' state. The revolution survived the assault, but at a terrible price. By 1922, as a result of the civil war, famine stalked Russia, and the working class—the class that made the Russian Revolution—was decimated.

Neither Lenin nor any other leader of the Russian Revolution had any illusion that a workers' state could survive this barbarism without the support of a revolution in more advanced countries. The Russian revolutionaries believed that socialism could be started in Russia—but that it could only be finished after an international socialist revolution.

And in fact, a wave of upheavals did sweep across Europe following the Russian Revolution, toppling monarchies in Germany and the Austro-Hungarian empire and shaking societies around the globe. But workers didn't succeed in taking power anywhere else for any length of time. So the Russian Revolution was left isolated.

In these desperate circumstances, Russia's shattered working class couldn't continue to exercise power through workers' councils. More and more, decisions were made by a group of state bureaucrats, led by Joseph Stalin. Eventually, Stalin and his allies struck out on their own. They began to make decisions on the basis of how to protect and increase their own power. Though continuing to use the rhetoric of socialism, they began to take back every gain won in the revolution—without exception. Control over the workplace was put in the hands of state-appointed managers. The Tsar's empire was rebuilt. Women lost their newfound rights.

This counterrevolution wasn't carried out without opposition. In particular, Leon Trotsky led the struggle to defend socialist principles. To finally consolidate power, Stalin had to murder or hound into exile every single surviving leader of the 1917 revolution.

Russia under Stalin became the opposite of the democratic workers' state of 1917. Though they mouthed socialist phrases, Stalin and the thugs who followed him ran a dictatorship where workers were every bit as exploited as in Western-style capitalist countries. They presided over a system of state capitalism—controlling society through state control over the economy.

Sadly, many people associate socialism with Stalin's tyranny—or with the top-down, undemocratic systems in China, Cuba and other so-called "socialist" countries modeled on the old USSR. That's certainly what supporters of capitalism encourage us to believe. After all, what better argument could there be against socialism than the idea that any attempt to win change is doomed to produce another Stalin? But Stalin's triumph in Russia wasn't inevitable. It was the result of a workers revolution left isolated in a sea of capitalism—strangled until it was finally defeated.

But none of this can erase what was accomplished by the revolution in Russia—the most backward society in Europe.

We're in a far more advanced position today—something made plain by the examples of workers' struggle since 1917. The history of the 20th century is filled with huge social explosions in which the struggles of workers took center stage. From France and Portugal in Europe, to Iran in the Middle East, to Chile in South America, to Poland under the thumb of the Stalinist dictatorship in Eastern Europe, these upheavals—along with dozens of others—showed the power of workers to shake the status quo and pose an alternative.

Though they failed to establish socialism, these revolutionary upheavals brought the mass of the population to life. And that is what socialism is about—a society created by the vast majority and organized around what they want it to be. As the British author of children's books Arthur Ransome wrote of the new world he witnessed in revolutionary Russia:

> We have seen the flight of the young eagles. Nothing can destroy that fact, even if, later in the day, the eagles fall to earth one by one, with broken wings...These men who have made the Soviet government in Russia, if they must fail, will fail with clean shields and clean hearts, having striven for an ideal which will live beyond them. Even if they fail, they will nonetheless have written a page of history more daring than any other which I can remember in the history of humanity.

Why You Should Be a Socialist

"So many people have been doing so well for so long."
That's how Peter Jennings of ABC News introduced a report on the U.S. economy in the spring of 1999. It's a line
that's heard often in the mainstream media. The picture
they paint is of a society grown fat and happy after years of
the U.S. economy steaming ahead. And it's no surprise
coming from the likes of Peter Jennings. Like the other
big-shot journalists, he would rather celebrate the good
fortune of people like himself—the minority that reaped
the benefits of the "miracle" economy.

But there's another side to the story.

For a majority of the U.S. population, the quality of life
is deteriorating—for some, very quickly. Anyone who's
waited in an overflowing doctor's office or watched their
high-interest credit card debt mount or faced added pres-
sures at even a low-paying, mindless job knows what Peter
Jennings doesn't about this society. And this underbelly of
the U.S. "miracle" economy is reflected in even more ugly
ways around the globe—terrible poverty, bloody wars and
violence, political repression and ecological catastrophes.

All this has contributed to a deep pool of anger and bitterness among all the people who recognize that the system works for the rich—but not for them.

For years, this anger bubbled away beneath the surface. Far more often than ever got reported, it was expressed outwardly—in demonstrations, in strikes, in boycotts and petitioning, in action of all sorts. But often, the protests were small. They didn't involve people beyond those personally connected to a particular issue—and therefore others who might have participated never heard of them.

But more and more, the bitterness is bubbling over. At the end of November 1999, tens of thousands of people took to the streets of Seattle to protest the World Trade Organization. The demonstrators came from all sorts of backgrounds—unionists, students, environmentalists, anti-sweatshop activists. Many had never worked together before, but they were united in their determination—even in the face of unprovoked police attacks—to show that they were fed up with corporate greed. Around the world, people watched the protests and sympathized with the demonstrators.

The Peter Jennings of the world were stunned. Where had these people come from? Why didn't they understand that the free market was in their best interests? A few commentators turned to the tried-and-true tactic of slander. Anti-WTO protesters were "a Noah's ark of flat-earth advocates, protectionist trade unions and yuppies looking for their 1960s fix," wrote the obnoxious Thomas Friedman of the *New York Times*.

But not even Friedman's colleagues bought that one. For a few days, the media had to acknowledge the issues that brought demonstrators to Seattle. They carried stories about corporate layoffs in the midst of an economic boom, the menace of genetically modified food, sweatshop working conditions both abroad and inside the U.S., environmental regulations gutted by governments around the world and animal species driven into extinction for the sake of profit.

Naturally, the media's attention quickly shifted back to the wonders of Wall Street and the wealth of the new Internet millionaires. But the anger hasn't gone away.

The battle in Seattle was one in a series of events that, taken together, show the development of a growing resistance to the priorities of this rotten system. A week before the anti-WTO demonstrations, more than 10,000 people "crossed the line" at Fort Benning, Ga., to protest the School of the Americas, the Pentagon's notorious training ground for Latin American dictators and death squads. The movement against sweatshop labor conditions continued to spread to new college campuses around the country.

The next month, South Carolina civil rights groups were hoping for a turnout of 20,000 to protest the racist Confederate flag that flies over the state house—they were shocked when close to 50,000 people came from miles around to demonstrate. Around the same time, Florida Gov. Jeb Bush was sparking a revolt by proposing to scrap affirmative action—thousands of people marched and rallied to show their opposition. And in Illinois, years of pressure and protest forced Illinois Gov. George Ryan to call a halt to executions—a tremendous victory over a corrupt and barbaric death-penalty system that has released 13 innocent men from the state's death row in the past 13 years.

And these are only the highlights. In a system based on inequality and injustice, there are issues in every corner of society that spark outrage—and need to be organized around. But whether there's action—whether the protests get called, whether the petitions are circulated, whether the transportation is organized and the signs get made—

depends on what people decide to do.

This is where politics matter. We may be witnessing a developing resistance, but it comes after more than two decades of defeats for organizations of working people. This has had an impact on how people organize themselves to fight—even whether they fight.

The labor movement, for example, has been hammered by employer attacks that pushed down the percentage of union workers in this country to a low of 13.9 percent. In the face of this offensive, union leaders have argued that strikes and militant action are methods of the past that do more harm than good. Instead, they've devoted massive sums and vast resources to winning favor in Washington as their strategy for defending union rights. The result today is that, while strikes like the 1997 United Parcel Service walkout showed the power of workers, there are competing ideas about how unions should flex their muscle.

So who's right? Are strikes outdated? Do militant tactics alienate our allies? Will the Democrats serve our interests? What are the bosses up to today? What strategies can help us win?

These are political questions that have to be answered. How they get answered will shape the struggles of the future—ultimately, whether they win or lose.

In this sense, politics don't just belong to the politicians and the media commentators or even union leaders and heads of civil rights and liberal organizations. Politics belong to all of us—because how we answer political questions helps to decide what happens in society.

A Revolutionary Socialist Party

Ideas can change very quickly in struggle. But they don't change all at once. In every battle, there are arguments over what to do next. Some people will see the need to step up the struggle—and to make the link to other political issues. Other people will argue that militant action makes matters worse. The outcome of the arguments shapes the outcome of the struggle.

This is where the intervention of socialists—who can express the experience of past struggles and suggest a way forward—is crucial. An organization of socialists can unite people so they can share their experiences and hammer out an understanding of how to fight back from day to day—in a workplace or a community or at a school. The strength of such an organization is in the range of experiences and the political understanding of all its members.

None of this would be much use to a political party like the Democrats. The Democratic Party exists for one reason—to get Democrats elected to office. For that, it needs its supporters once or twice every couple years—to turn out to vote.

Socialists have very different goals—so our political party will have to look very different. We need socialists in every workplace to agitate around fightbacks on the shop floor. We need socialists in every neighborhood to take up the questions of housing and police violence and health care and everything else that comes up. We need students to agitate on college campuses. We need socialists in every corner of society inhabited by working people, and we need these socialists working nonstop—organizing struggle and carrying on political discussions.

This commitment to struggle is part of our socialist tradition. Socialists have always been at the forefront of the fight for a better world. They have been leaders in the union movement, in the movement against racism, in the fight against war and many others.

To achieve its aims, a revolutionary socialist organization has to be more democratic than other political organizations under capitalism. We need to bring together the experiences of every socialist—and to make those experiences part of the common basis that we all organize on.

But a socialist organization has to be centralized—to be prepared to act together in the fight against the bosses. Why the need for a centralized organization? Because the other side is organized. The basis of their power is the profit they make at the workplace—highly organized systems built around exploiting workers. Their side organizes political propaganda through the media. Their side responds to resistance with a highly organized and disciplined police force and army.

We need an organization for our side—one that can coordinate actions not just in one workplace or even one city but around the country. We need an organization that can put forward a common set of ideas—using its own newspapers and magazines and books. Socialists have to be able to fight around the same program, whether they're teachers or autoworkers or college students, and whether they live in Chicago or New York or Los Angeles—and ultimately Seoul or London or Johannesburg.

The bigger the struggle, the more complex and urgent the political questions. In the Russian Revolution of 1917, the hated Tsar was toppled in a matter of a few days. That part of the revolution was almost completely spontaneous. No socialist organization picked the date for the demonstrations that snowballed into a mass movement. The accumulated hatred for the Tsar and his regime was all that was necessary.

But the issue of what came next raised questions that couldn't be answered with spontaneous action. The government that came to power after the Tsar included people who called themselves socialists—and who claimed that the revolution had to be demobilized for the people's victories to be consolidated. Were they right? What should be done to make sure the Tsar never came to power again? How could democracy and justice be spread even further? Should they?

These questions were hotly debated throughout Russian society. The reason they were ultimately given socialist answers is because a tried-and-tested revolutionary socialist organization existed to make its case. On the basis of its past experience and its roots among workers across Russia, the Bolshevik Party was able to recognize and make sense of the situation in all its complexity—and express the aims of socialism that workers favored.

Sadly, the need for socialist organization has been proven many times since—but in the negative. Too many times, mass mobilizations of workers threw the status quo into question—only to allow it back in because socialists weren't in a position to make the case for how to go forward.

Such an organization doesn't form overnight. It spends decades preparing itself to be a voice at the crucial time.

This, then, is the case for why you should be a socialist. As individuals on our own, we can't accomplish much—not even with the best grasp of what's wrong with the world and how it could be different. But as part of an organization, we can make a difference.

This isn't an abstract question. There are towns in the Midwest where Ku Klux Klan members no longer parade around because socialists took the initiative to shut them down. There are former death-row prisoners who are alive today because socialists, along with others, drew attention to their cases and helped to show why they shouldn't be executed—because they were innocent. There are workplaces where supervisors can't get away with murder because individual socialists stood up to them. Socialists can and do make a difference right now.

We need to make more of a difference. We need socialists in every workplace, on every campus, in every neighborhood—involved in every struggle throughout society.

But there's a further task. Socialists need to show how the day-to-day fights of today are part of a long-term fight for bigger political changes. As Marx and Engels put it more than 150 years ago: "The Communists fight for the attainment of the immediate aims, for the enforcement of the momentary interests of the working class; but in the movement of the present, they also represent and take care of the future of that movement."

Socialists are among the best fighters in the struggles of today. But we're also involved in the struggle for the future—ultimately, for a different kind of society where exploitation and oppression are never known again. That is the vision of a society that we put forward—and the struggle to make that vision open to larger numbers of people is the way that socialists put the best of themselves forward.

We live in a rotten and barbaric world. For huge numbers of people, just surviving from day to day is intolerably difficult. For the rest of the vast majority, the struggle to get by leaves almost no time for leisure—much less putting our minds to making the world a better place to live in. Capitalism has produced poverty, famine, environmental catastrophe and bloody wars.

To hear defenders of the system explain it, these horrors are inevitable. It may not be a perfect world, we're told, but it's the best we can do.

What a sick society it is which tells us that 6 million children dead of malnutrition each year is the best we can do. That more than 1.5 million Iraqis killed by economic sanctions is the best we can do. That a world threatened by ecological devastation is the best we can do.

We don't have to pay that price. The resources exist to eliminate all these horrors—and build a socialist society free of poverty and oppression where we all have control over our lives.

That is a world worth fighting for.

Eugene V. Debs and the Idea of Socialism
An Afterword
by Howard Zinn

We are always in need of radicals who are also lovable, and
so we would do well to remember Eugene Victor Debs.
Ninety years ago, and the time *The Progressive* was born,
Debs was nationally famous as leader of the Socialist Party,
and the poet James Witcomb Riley wrote of him:

> As warm a heart as ever beat
> Betwixt here and the Judgment Seat.

Debs was what every socialist or anarchist or radical
should be: fierce in his convictions, kind and compassion-
ate in his personal relations. Sam Moore, a fellow inmate of
the Atlanta penitentiary, where Debs was imprisoned for
opposing the First World War, remembered how he felt as
Debs was about to be released on Christmas Day, 1921:

Howard Zinn is author of *A People's History of the United States.*
This article first appeared in *The Progressive* January 1999, and
is reprinted here with permission from both the author and the
magazine.

> As miserable as I was, I would defy fate with all its cruelty as long as Debs held my hand, and I was the most miserably happiest man on Earth when I knew he was going home Christmas.

Debs had won the hearts of his fellow prisoners in Atlanta. He had fought for them in a hundred ways and refused any special privileges for himself. On the day of his release, the warden ignored prison regulations and opened every cellblock to allow more than 2,000 inmates to gather in front of the main jail building to say goodbye to Eugene Debs. As he started down the walkway from the prison, a roar went up and he turned, tears streaming down his face, and stretched out his arms to the other prisoners.

This was not his first prison experience. In 1894, not yet a socialist but an organizer for the American Railway Union, he had led a nationwide boycott of the railroads in support of the striking workers at the Pullman Palace Car Company. They tied up the railroad system, burned hundreds of railway cars, and were met with the full force of the capitalist state: Attorney General Richard Olney, a former railroad lawyer, got a court injunction to prohibit blocking trains. President Cleveland called out the army, which used bayonets and rifle fire on a crowd of 5,000 strike sympathizers in Chicago. Seven hundred were arrested. Thirteen were shot to death.

Debs was jailed for violating an injunction prohibiting him from doing or saying anything to carry on the strike. In court, he denied he was a socialist, but during his six months in prison he read socialist literature, and the events of the strike took on a deeper meaning. He wrote later:

> I was to be baptized in socialism in the roar of conflict. In the gleam of every bayonet and the flash of every rifle the class struggle was revealed.

From then on, Debs devoted his life to the cause of working people and the dream of a socialist society. He stood on the platform with Mother Jones and Big Bill Haywood in 1905 at the founding convention of the Industrial Workers of the World. He was a magnificent speaker, his long body leaning forward from the podium, his arm raised dramatically. Thousands came to hear him talk all over the country.

With the outbreak of war in Europe in 1914 and the build-up of war fever against Germany, some socialists succumbed to the talk of "preparedness," but Debs was adamantly opposed. When President Wilson and Congress brought the nation into the war in 1917, speech was no longer free. The Espionage Act made it a crime to say anything that would discourage enlistment in the armed forces.

Soon, close to 1,000 people were in prison for protesting the war. The producer of a movie called *The Spirit of '76*, about the American revolution, was sentenced to ten years in prison for promoting anti-British feeling at a time when England and the United States were allies. The case was officially labeled *The U.S. v. The Spirit of '76*.

Debs made a speech in Canton, Ohio, in support of the men and women in jail for opposing the war. He told his listeners:

> Wars throughout history have been waged for conquest and plunder. And that is war, in a nutshell. The master class has always declared the wars; the subject class has always fought the battles.

He was found guilty and sentenced to ten years in prison by a judge who denounced those "who would strike the sword from the hand of the nation while she is engaged in defending herself against a foreign and brutal power."

In court, Debs refused to call any witnesses, declaring:

"I have been accused of obstructing the war. I admit it. I abhor war. I would oppose war if I stood alone." Before sentencing, Debs spoke to judge and jury, uttering perhaps his most famous words. I was in his hometown of Terre Haute, Indiana, recently, among 200 people gathered to honor his memory, and we began the evening by reciting those words—words that moved me deeply when I first read them and move me deeply still:

> While there is a lower class, I am in it. While there is a criminal element, I am of it. While there is a soul in prison, I am not free.

The "liberal" Oliver Wendell Holmes, speaking for a unanimous Supreme Court, upheld the verdict, on the ground that Debs's speech was intended to obstruct military recruiting. When the war as over, the "liberal" Woodrow Wilson turned down his Attorney General's recommendation that Debs be released, even though he was sixty-five and in poor health. Debs was in prison for thirty-two months. Finally, in 1921, the Republican Warren Harding ordered him freed on Christmas Day.

Today, when capitalism, "the free market," and "private enterprise" are being hailed as triumphant in the world, it is a good time to remember Debs and to rekindle the idea of socialism.

To see the disintegration of the Soviet Union as a sign of the failure of socialism is to mistake the monstrous tyranny created by Stalin for the vision of an egalitarian and democratic society that has inspired enormous numbers of people all over the world. Indeed, the removal of the Soviet Union as the false surrogate for the idea of socialism creates a great opportunity. We can now reintroduced genuine socialism to a world feeling the sickness of capitalism—its nationalist hatreds, its perpetual warfare, riches for a small number of people in a small number of countries, and hunger, homelessness, insecurity for everyone else.

Here in the United States we should recall that enthusiasm for socialism—production for use instead of profit, economic and social equality, solidarity with our brothers and sisters all over the world—was at its height before the Soviet Union came into being.

In the era of Debs, the first seventeen years of the twentieth century—until war created an opportunity to crush the movement—millions of Americans declared their adherence to the principles of socialism. Those were years of bitter labor struggles, the great walkouts of women garment workers in New York, the victorious multi-ethnic strike of textile workers in Lawrence, Massachusetts, the unbelievable courage of coal miners in Colorado, defying the power and wealth of the Rockefellers. The I.W.W. was born—revolutionary, militant, demanding "one big union" for everyone, skilled and unskilled, black and white, men and women, native-born and foreign-born.

More than a million people read *Appeal to Reason* and other socialist newspapers. In proportion to population, it would be as if today more than three million Americans read a socialist press. The party had 100,000 members, and 1,200 office-holders in 340 municipalities. Socialism was especially strong in the Southwest, among tenant farmers, railroad workers, coal miners, lumberjacks. Oklahoma had 12,000 dues-paying members in 1914 and more than 100 socialists in local offices. It was the home of the fiery Kate Richards O'Hare. Jailed for opposing the war, she once hurled a book through the skylight to bring fresh air into the foul-smelling jail block, bringing cheers from her fellow inmates.

The point of recalling all this is to remind us of the powerful appeal of the socialist idea to people alienated from the political system and aware of the growing stark disparities in income and wealth—as so many Americans are today. The word itself—"socialism"—may still carry the distortions of recent experience in bad places usurping the name. But any one who goes around the country, or reads carefully the public opinion surveys over the past decade, can see that huge numbers of Americans agree on what should be the fundamental elements of a decent society: guaranteed food, housing, medical care for everyone; bread and butter as better guarantees of "national security" than guns and bombs; democratic control of corporate power; equal rights for all races, genders, and sexual orientations; a recognition of the rights of immigrants as the unrecognized counterparts of our parents and grandparents; the rejection of war and violence as solutions for tyranny and injustice.

There are people fearful of the word, all along the political spectrum. What is important, I think, is not the word, but a determination to hold up before a troubled public those ideas that are both bold and inviting—the more bold, the more inviting. That's what remembering Debs and the socialist idea can do for us.

Further reading

I think the most important reading material of all is *Socialist Worker,* the newspaper of the International Socialist Organization. *SW* comes out every two weeks, crammed to the bursting point with news, political analysis, stories about the history of our movement and reports of struggle. Of course, I may be biased since I've worked on *SW* for the past 16 years. A lot of the information and arguments in this book first appeared in its pages (almost always written by someone other than me). I owe a great debt to the people who've written for *Socialist Worker* and devoted their enormous talents to producing it.

The *International Socialist Review* was launched only a few years ago, but I think it's already become the best left-wing journal around. The *ISR* comes out every two months, and it's an indispensable source for political discussion, analysis and debate.

If the arguments in this book aren't from *SW* or the *ISR,* there's a good chance they came from two wonderful books on socialism—Paul Foot's *Why You Should Join the Socialists* and John Molyneux's *Arguments for Revolutionary Socialism.* Unfortunately, both these books are out of print, but stray copies can sometimes be found on ISO literature tables—or borrowed from ISO members.

Two other essential introductory books about socialism

are by Chris Harman. *How Marxism Works* is a clear and concise account of the basic ideas of the Marxist tradition, and *Economics of the Madhouse* explains why the free market system fails so miserably.

The best introduction to Marxism was written by Marx. The 150-year-old *Communist Manifesto* reads as if it only arrived from the printer last week. Likewise, Lenin's short book *State and Revolution* should be the first stop for anyone who wants to understand how society can be changed. Rosa Luxemburg's *Reform or Revolution* makes the case as clearly as anyone ever has for why capitalism can't be reformed.

For the history of the U.S.'s rich tradition of struggle, *A People's History of the U.S.* by Howard Zinn is a good place to start. Sharon Smith's upcoming book *American Labor at the Crossroads* will collect arguments she's made in numerous articles that are crucial for understanding the politics of the U.S. working-class movement. On Black history, the starting point for socialists should be Ahmed Shawki's *Black Liberation and Socialism in the United States* in *International Socialism Journal 47*.

There's a lot to read about the Russian Revolution. Your first book should be *Ten Days That Shook the World,* an eyewitness account by the American journalist and socialist John Reed. Leon Trotsky's *History of the Russian Revolution* is more than 1,200 pages long, but every page is worth the read. Also, Tony Cliff's multi-volume political biographies of *Lenin* and *Trotsky* are excellent guides to the ideas of these two revolutionary leaders and the events they participated in.

Most of these books and publications are available from Bookmarks. For more information, write to: Bookmarks, P.O. Box 16085, Chicago, IL 60616. Or call 773-665-9601.

Socialist Worker
Newspaper of the International Socialist Organization

In every issue of *Socialist Worker,* you get eyewitness reports and interviews covering struggles around the world—plus political analysis of the issues we face every day. All it costs is $25 for a one-year subscription—25 biweekly issues. Send your check or money order to: *Socialist Worker,* P.O. Box 16085, Chicago, IL 60616.

International Socialist Review
Journal of Revolutionary Marxism

International Socialism Journal takes on the key discussions and debates of the working-class movement—and explains how the world around us works. A one-year subscription gets you six issues for the cost of $30. Send your check or money order to: *International Socialist Review,* P.O. Box 258082, Chicago, IL 60625.

Join the ISO

If you like what you read in this book, you need to join the International Socialist Organization. We have branches and members in cities across the country. If you want to join the ISO—or if you simply want to know more about us—contact the ISO national office. You can write to: ISO, P.O. Box 16085, Chicago, IL 60616. Or call 773-665-7337. Or visit our Web site at www.internationalsocialist.org.